IN THE MICROWAVE

Sumptuous Sauces
IN THE MICROWAVE

PATRICIA TENNISON

CB
CONTEMPORARY
BOOKS
CHICAGO · NEW YORK

Library of Congress Cataloging-in-Publication Data

Tennison, Patricia.
   Sumptuous sauces in the microwave.

   Includes index.
   1. Microwave cookery.   2. Sauces.   I. Title.
TX832.T46   1989   641.8′14   88-36219
ISBN 0-8092-4419-5

Published by Contemporary Books, Inc.
180 North Michigan Avenue, Chicago, Illinois 60601
Manufactured in the United States of America
Library of Congress Catalog Card Number: 88-36219
International Standard Book Number: 0-8092-4419-5

Published simultaneously in Canada by Beaverbooks, Ltd.
195 Allstate Parkway, Valleywood Business Park
Markham, Ontario L3R 4T8 Canada

This book is dedicated to my family—
my husband, Tom, and our children, Jeff and Ashley—
and to the opportunity to touch the future—
for this is how our children's children will be cooking.

CONTENTS

INTRODUCTION

What is a sauce? First, let's talk about what it is not: it is not necessarily fatty, and it is not meant to disguise poor-quality food.

A fine sauce is thyme, rosemary, and wine; or tomatoes, basil, and olive oil; or butter, flour, and milk; or fish bones simmered in wine. It is a moist accompaniment, often based on the juices of meats or vegetables.

Some of the most healthful foods we eat, such as pasta, cry out for an equally appealing sauce to make Monday's spaghetti differ from Thursday's linguine. A hot vinaigrette enlivens a tossed salad. Fresh raspberries and a touch of sugar turn into a guilt-free sauce in the microwave.

I've made liberal use of the word *sauces* in this book to include marinades, warm salad dressings, and spicy fruit purees, as well as classic white sauces, colorful pasta sauces, old-fashioned gravies, and fresh-fruit dessert toppings.

In each chapter, sauces typically are arranged from the simplest to the most complex. Where possible, lower-fat versions are offered. For example, there are two versions of veloute. Classic Veloute is a luscious, rich sauce based on cream. Low-Fat Veloute is a fine, thick sauce that becomes creamlike by reduction.

Also included at the end of the book is a helpful listing of food and sauce pairings. This extensive list provides suggestions for sauces to accompany everything from meat and fish, vegetables and pasta, to desserts.

Why use sauces? When you have cooked vegetables, fish, or meat, a sauce makes good use of the resulting natural juices. Nothing is wasted, and if you thicken the sauce by using cornstarch or by reducing, little fat is added. A colorful sauce adds interest to a well-arranged dinner plate. An unexpected sauce anoints leftovers. And some treats—such as homemade chicken gravy over mashed potatoes or hot fudge sauce over ice cream—just plain taste good.

A good cook should know how to make a béchamel—the French term for basic white sauce. And with a few twists of ingredients, a humble béchamel turns into a Mornay, Basil Cream, Creamy Garlic, or even Goat Cheese sauce.

Most of the sauces in this book can be made ahead, on the weekends, so that the refrigerator could hold a Mediterranean Olive sauce for fettuccine, Sour and Sweet dressing for a salad, Clarified Butter for lobster, homemade Texas Sharp Barbecue sauce for ribs, classic Béarnaise for steak, and side dishes of Lemon-Orange Cranberry sauce or Mango Chutney to highlight future meals.

Why use the microwave for sauces? That's the easiest question. First, the microwave saves time. Delicate sauces don't stick to the pan. Cleanup is a breeze. The microwave helps keep the kitchen cool in the summer. And sauces can be made in a convenient glass container that is easy to pour and then place right in the dishwasher.

When sauces become this easy to make, you'll find that you make them more often. Meals become more varied, and dining becomes an even greater pleasure.

PART I
THE BASICS

1

THE MICROWAVE

For many of us, switching to a microwave oven feels like starting over. It takes a little time—and a little courage. Rest assured that many of the tenets of fine cooking remain the same. Food will taste best if you start with the freshest ingredients. You'll still need to melt some butter, whip a sauce, taste for herbs, and test for texture. The microwave just lets you move faster.

Microwaves are short radio waves. The waves themselves are not hot; that is, they do not give off heat like charcoal on a grill or like an electric coil that heats air in a conventional oven.

Instead, microwaves pass through many materials, such as glass, ceramic, paper, and most plastic, without causing heat. That is why you can cook food in a glass bowl in a microwave and still find the bowl cool enough to handle.

However, microwaves are absorbed by water, sugar, starches, and fats. Microwaves excite water molecules, and when the molecules move, the friction causes heat, just as rubbing your hands together causes heat.

The magnetron tube in a microwave oven works like a broadcasting station, sending out the waves. The waves travel in a straight line, bouncing off metal walls and any fans designed to move the waves within a microwave oven.

It is important that you never operate your microwave oven when it is empty, or the microwaves could damage the magnetron tube.

Microwaves penetrate about ⅓ inch to 1½ inches into foods, depending on the density of the food. This outer inch of food heats up, and the heat transfers to cook the rest of the food. Some foods need to be stirred or rearranged so that the microwaves can reach uncooked portions.

COOKING TIMES

Recipes in this book were tested in microwave ovens that operate on 600 to 700 watts. Cooking times are approximate because microwave ovens vary by manufacturer. Small or early models generally have lower wattage and require longer cooking time; check your machine's manual.

Common power settings are not yet standardized. As a guide, however, *high* means 100 percent power or full power, *medium-high* is 70 percent power, *medium* is 50 percent or half power, *defrost* is 30 percent power, and *warm* is 10 percent power.

EQUIPMENT

Your cupboards probably already contain enough equipment to get you started.

Glass, ceramic, and plastic bowls and dishes are best. Microwaves pass through these materials. To test to see if a favorite plate or bowl is microwave-proof, put it in the microwave next to a glass measure filled with a cup of cool water. Microwave on high power for one minute. If the water is warm but the plate you are testing feels cool to the touch, the plate is fine for the microwave. If the plate feels slightly warm, you could use it to reheat foods but not for long cooking. If the plate feels hot, do not use it in the microwave.

Do not use metal pans, gold- or silver-rimmed plates, or utensils with screws or metal handles. Microwaves will be reflected off the metals and may damage the oven. Delicate glassware and china are not recommended.

Even if dishes are suitable for the microwave, heat may transfer from the cooked food and make the container too hot to handle. Use oven mitts when removing dishes from the microwave.

Just as with conventional cooking, recipes work best if you use cooking equipment of the recommended size. If a bowl is too large, the food will spread out and may cook unevenly. If a bowl is too small, certain foods, especially sauces, may overflow.

Most of the sauces in this book can be made if you have two- and four-cup measures, a two-quart covered casserole, a three-quart bowl, plastic or wooden spoons, and a whisk.

COVERING TECHNIQUES

Covering holds in heat and moisture, helping foods to cook faster and more evenly in the microwave. When a recipe says "cover," use a tight-fitting lid or plastic wrap. When using plastic wrap, fold back a corner to create a vent; this helps prevent the wrap from splitting and also makes it possible to stir food without removing the wrap.

Take care when removing covers. Open casseroles and remove plastic wrap by lifting the far corner. This allows hot steam to escape and helps you avoid burns.

Many of the sauce recipes require no cover, especially at the end of the cooking time. This allows moisture to evaporate so that the sauce will thicken and intensify in flavor.

TIPS

Be sure to read your oven's manual for specific instructions and read each recipe through once before you start cooking. Here are some general tips:

- Many wooden spoons can be left right in the bowl when you are cooking in the microwave and remain cool to the touch. However, I find that old wooden spoons that have darkened from age and oil do get quite hot. Experiment carefully.
- A larger mass of food takes longer to cook in the microwave.
- Stir cooked, outside portions to the inside.
- Check your measuring spoons. Many measuring spoons, particularly inexpensive ones purchased in supermarkets, are not standard sizes,

and the difference can be dramatic, especially when baking or making sauces. Look for the initials *US STD* (U.S. Standard) on the largest spoon in the set. If you don't find these words or initials on your favorite measuring spoons, find a friend or friendly storekeeper who has such a set. Measure a level tablespoon of salt using the standard set, and see if that salt fills your own tablespoon exactly. Repeat with the rest of the set.

- Spoons, whisks, and measures can get very sticky when working with wet flour. For easier cleaning, rinse the utensils immediately in lukewarm water. Hot water will cause the starch in the flour to cook to a sticky glue.
- Use the whisk rather than a wooden spoon for white sauces, veloutes, and Hollandaise. It does a better job at fighting lumps.
- To store most sauces, cover and store up to a week in the refrigerator. The longer sauce stands, the thicker it becomes as it loses moisture.
- To reheat most sauces, microwave on medium power until warm. If sauce has thickened during storage, first stir in a teaspoon of water or milk.
- To reduce fat, butter may be omitted from stocks and margarine substituted in many sauces. Although it adds flavor and helps create a creamy texture, butter is not needed in the microwave to keep food from sticking to the cooking dish.

2
INGREDIENTS AND TERMS

GUIDE TO INGREDIENTS

Butter: The recipes in this book use unsalted butter, also called sweet butter. This butter has no added salt.

Capers: Pickled flower buds of a Mediterranean shrub. They add a piquant flavor to dishes.

Cornstarch: Tasteless, white powdery starch made from corn. It is typically blended with a little liquid to form a smooth paste, then added to sauce to help it thicken.

Cream: Half-and-half, which is a mixture of milk and cream, has up to 18 percent milk fat; light whipping cream, 30 percent to 36 percent milk fat; heavy whipping cream, 36 percent to 40 percent milk fat.

Eggs: Recipes in this book use grade A large eggs.

Green onions: Long, skinny onions, also called spring onions or scallions, with small white bulbs and long greens. The bulb and first two inches of the green are tender enough to use in most dishes. Save the tougher green ends for stocks.

Lemon: Use fresh lemons for lemon juice. The flavor is much better than the medicinal taste from bottled lemon juice. You will get more juice from a fresh lemon if you first heat it for about 10 seconds in the microwave.

Margarine: Butter substitute made from vegetable oils or animal fats, or both.

Milk: Whole milk has about 3 percent milk fat. Skim milk has less than 1 percent fat but all the protein and minerals of whole milk. Many nutritionists stress using skim milk to reduce fat. You may use skim milk in sauces, but the texture will be less creamy.

Mustard, dry: Powdered seed of the mustard plant. It is sold in jars or tins next to the dried herbs.

Mustard, prepared: Dry mustard mixed with vinegar, perhaps wine, and seasonings. American mustards often have turmeric added to give it a vibrant yellow color.

Oil: Unless specified, this means a light-flavored oil such as safflower. The flavor of peanut oil is too distinctive for most sauces. If the recipe calls for olive oil, particularly in a vinaigrette, using extra virgin olive oil will give a richer, deeper flavor.

Rind: Thin, outer layers of citrus, such as lemon or orange. The rind contains the oils of the fruit and its sharp taste. Remove rind with a very sharp paring knife or a zester. Avoid the bitter, white pith.

Shallot: A small bulb similar to an onion but with an aromatic, slightly garlic flavor.

Sour cream: Homogenized cream with added lactic acid culture that gives it a pleasant tang. Most stores also carry a lower-fat sour half-and-half, which also works well in sauces.

Stock or broth: Homemade beef, chicken, veal, fish, or vegetable stock is ideal, and recipes are included in the Stocks and Roux chapter. However, the same amount of good-quality canned or dry, cubed broth can be substituted. Usually these products will have plenty of salt, so taste the resulting sauce before adding salt and pepper.

Wine: The rule of thumb is to cook only with wines that are good enough to drink. Avoid so-called cooking wines. Be sparing—the wine should not overpower the sauce. Most of the alcohol will evaporate during the cooking process.

COOKING TERMS

Here are some basic cooking terms and their definitions as they apply to making sauces.

Beat: Blend ingredients together using a fork, spoon, or whisk in an over-and-over motion.

Blend: Mix into a smooth texture.

Brown: Cook until brown, such as butter or onions.

Chop: Cut into small pieces, not as small or regular as diced.

Dice: Cut into small cubes, about $\frac{1}{4}$-inch square. Diced foods are smaller than chopped but not as fine as minced.

Melt: Change from a solid to a liquid by heating.

Mince: Cut very fine, smaller than chopped or diced.

Puree: Make finely textured, like baby food. This is usually done using a fine sieve, food mill, food processor, or blender.

Reduce: Decrease the volume of a liquid by heating until some of the moisture evaporates. This intensifies flavors and thickens the sauce.

Skim: To remove fat or scum from the top of a stock or sauce. A large spoon will do the trick. Or let the stock chill, then remove hardened fat.

Stir: Gently mix to combine ingredients, using a spoon in a round-and-round movement.

Strain: Put through a sieve or finely woven cloth, such as cheesecloth, to remove solid materials.

Whip: Beat rapidly with a fork or beater to lighten and to incorporate air.

Whisk: Use a whisk to beat with a whiplike wrist action. It is the best way to remove lumps in flour-based sauces.

PART II
THE RECIPES

3

STOCKS AND ROUX

A good stock is the start of many fine sauces and soups. Once you get in the habit of buying an extra chicken on sale, freezing leftover fish bones, or looking at vegetable scraps with a creative eye, making beautiful stocks becomes almost effortless in the microwave.

Note that stocks first are cooked on high power until boiling, then on medium power to develop flavor. Cutting vegetables quite small also helps contribute flavor to the stocks.

Roux (pronounced roo) is a simple combination of cooked butter and flour that is used as a base for sauces, gravy, and soup.

When cooked conventionally, on the stove, care must be taken not to let the roux burn on the bottom of the pan. However, this is less likely to happen in the microwave oven because the roux is cooked evenly from all sides.

I like to use a 4-cup glass measure when making roux. The glass makes it easy to see what you are cooking, and the handle makes the measure easy to carry. The size is ample for whisking, and there is room for plenty of liquid if you are preceding right into a sauce.

Make White Roux for light-colored sauces and Brown Roux for robust, dark sauces. Roux will keep for weeks covered in the refrigerator.

WHITE STOCK

A roaster chicken will give a deeper flavor, but a fine stock can be made with a simple fryer. Add all the skin, plus any extra skins that you may have removed and frozen. They contribute extra flavor, and the fat from the skin is easy to remove after the stock is refrigerated.

Don't use livers for White Stock; the flavor is much too strong. And I don't use chicken hearts either, because I find the flavor too beefy for White Stock.

White Stock is cooked on high power until boiling, then on medium to develop flavor.

Preparation time: 15 minutes
Microwave time: 1 hour 21 minutes–1 hour 38 minutes
Yield: 2½ cups

> 3 pounds chicken, chicken parts, or
>   meaty chicken or veal bones
> 1 carrot, chopped coarse
> 1 small onion, quartered
> 2 celery ribs with fresh yellow leaves,
>   chopped coarse
> ¼ cup chopped fresh parsley
> 1 bay leaf, crushed
> 6 peppercorns
> ¼ teaspoon dried thyme
> 4 cups water

1. Put all ingredients in a 3-quart casserole. Cover tightly with plastic or lid. MICROWAVE (high) 18–20 minutes, until boiling. Skim off and discard foam. Turn over or rearrange chicken.
2. Cover again. MICROWAVE (high) 3 minutes, until broth returns to boil. MICROWAVE (medium) 1–1¼ hours, until flavors develop. Strain. Use a

large spoon to skim off fat. Or, if you have time, first refrigerate the stock to make it easier to remove all the fat.

TIP: Pick the meat off the bones after using for stock and save for soup or sandwiches.

WHITE ROUX

White Roux is a simple blend of butter and flour, cooked long enough to rid the mixture of a "floury" taste. It is the first step of many fine sauces, soups, and gravies.

Preparation time: 1 minute
Microwave time: 3–5 minutes
Yield: 3 tablespoons

2 tablespoons butter
2 tablespoons flour

1. Put butter in a 4-cup measure. MICROWAVE (high) 1–2 minutes, until melted and hot.
2. Whisk in flour. MICROWAVE (high) 2–3 minutes, until flour is cooked through but mixture is still a light tan color. Whisk until smooth.

TIP: To make ¼ cup, put 4 tablespoons butter in a 4-cup measure. MICROWAVE (high) 1–2 minutes. Whisk in 4 tablespoons flour. MICROWAVE (high) 2–3 minutes. Whisk well.

BROWN STOCK

Brown Stock is one of those recipes where you need a conventional oven. Bones for the stock don't brown as well in the microwave, and pale, uncooked bones make a pale, thin-tasting stock. My solution is to brown the bones in a conventional oven, then use the microwave to speed up the rest of the cooking. If you want an all-microwave version, see the Quick Brown Stock recipe (see Index).

Oven roasting time: 1 hour
Preparation time: 15 minutes
Microwave time: 32–40 minutes
Yield: 3½ cups

  4 pounds beef marrow bones
  1 small onion, peeled and quartered
  2 celery ribs with fresh yellow leaves
  2 medium-sized carrots
  1 small turnip, trimmed
  1 tablespoon butter
  4 cups water
  1 cup chopped fresh or drained canned
    tomatoes
10 peppercorns
  ¼ cup chopped fresh parsley
  1 bay leaf, crushed
  1 teaspoon fresh thyme *or* ¼ teaspoon
    dried

1. Heat conventional oven to 350°F. Place bones on bottom of roasting pan and cook about 1 hour until brown, turning once.
2. Meanwhile, use a food processor or knife to finely chop onion, celery, carrots, and turnip. Put vegetables in a 3-quart casserole. Add butter. MICROWAVE (high) 4–5 minutes to soften, stirring after 1 minute.

3. Stir in rest of ingredients and the browned bones. Cover tightly. MICRO-WAVE (high) 18-20 minutes, until boiling, stirring after 10 minutes to rearrange bones. MICROWAVE (medium) 10-15 minutes, until flavors develop. Strain. Taste and add salt if needed.

BROWN ROUX

Brown Roux has the same ingredients as White Roux, but the butter and flour mixture is cooked longer until it reaches a rich brown color. A deeply colored roux plays an important role in Creole cooking, as well as in classic French brown sauces.

Preparation time: 1 minute
Microwave time: 5-7 minutes
Yield: 3 tablespoons

2 tablespoons butter
2 tablespoons flour

1. Put butter in a 4-cup measure. MICROWAVE (high) 1-2 minutes, until melted and hot.
2. Whisk in flour. MICROWAVE (high) 4-5 minutes, until flour is cooked through and mixture turns to a rich brown color.

TIP: To make ¼ cup, put 4 tablespoons butter in a 4-cup measure. MICROWAVE (high) 1-2 minutes. Whisk in 4 tablespoons flour. MICROWAVE (high) 8-9 minutes. Whisk well.

FISH STOCK

Turning worthless fish bones and fish heads into rich stock is one of the magical moments of cooking. And it makes small children respect your ways.

For a good-tasting stock, use the heads, bones, tails, and skin of the fish, rinsing very well to remove all blood. You should be able to get fish parts from a fish store for free or for a nominal charge. Light-flavored fish make the best-tasting stock. Avoid using salmon, sturgeon, buffalofish, and other strong-tasting fish.

The vegetables for this stock are chopped very fine—a food processor makes this easy—to get the most flavor during the short cooking time. The stock is cooked on high power to get the liquid boiling, then on medium power to let flavors develop.

Preparation time: 20 minutes
Microwave time: 32–36 minutes
Yield: 3 cups

1 small onion, peeled and quartered
2 peeled shallots
2 celery ribs with fresh yellow leaves
2 medium-sized carrots
1 tablespoon butter
6 peppercorns
¼ cup chopped fresh parsley
1 bay leaf, crushed
1 teaspoon fresh thyme *or* ¼ teaspoon dried
2 whole cloves
½ cup white wine
3½ cups water
2 pounds fish bones and heads, washed

1. Use a food processor or knife to finely chop onion, shallots, celery, and carrots. Put vegetables in a 3-quart casserole. Add butter. MICROWAVE (high) 4 minutes to soften, stirring after 1 minute.
2. Stir in rest of ingredients. Cover tightly. MICROWAVE (high) 18-20 minutes, until boiling, stirring after 10 minutes to rearrange bones. MICROWAVE (medium) 10-12 minutes, until flavors develop. Strain. Taste and add salt if needed.

TIP: To reduce fat, the tablespoon of butter may be omitted. You don't need it in the microwave to keep vegetables from sticking, but it does add flavor.

TIP: Keep Fish Stock in the refrigerator for up to four days or in the freezer for up to four weeks.

VEGETABLE STOCK

This stock likely will be different each time you make it, depending on the vegetables you have available that day. Use this recipe as a guide, freely adding onions, leeks, watercress, carrots, celery, and turnips. Use asparagus, mushrooms, spinach, and tomatoes sparingly to avoid overpowering the stock. Avoid strong vegetables such as cabbage, broccoli, and cauliflower.

The vegetables are chopped fine to help develop flavor. Be sure to taste the raw vegetables after they are chopped and combined but before they are cooked. The stock will taste very much like the raw vegetable mixture. If you have been experimenting with combinations and don't like the taste of the raw mixture, you won't like the stock. Bail out and start again.

Vegetable Stock is cooked on high power until boiling, then on medium to develop flavor.

Preparation time: 15 minutes
Microwave time: 53 minutes–1 hour 8 minutes
Yield: 2½ cups

> 1 teaspoon sugar
> 1 tablespoon butter
> ½ cup chopped onion or leek
> 2 medium carrots, trimmed, scraped if desired
> 1 small turnip, trimmed
> 3 celery ribs with fresh yellow leaves
> ½ cup mushroom stems
> ¼ cup fresh parsley
> 1 bay leaf, crushed
> 4 cups water

1. Put sugar, butter, and onion or leek in a 3-quart casserole. MICROWAVE (high) uncovered 8–10 minutes, until tender and light brown but not burned, stirring after 1 minute.
2. Use a knife or food processor to finely chop carrots, turnip, celery, mushroom stems, parsley, and bay leaf. Add to casserole. Add water. Cover tightly. MICROWAVE (high) 15–18 minutes, until boiling. Stir.
3. Cover again. MICROWAVE (medium) 30–40 minutes. Strain and squeeze vegetables well with a spoon to extract juices.

TIP: The stock will be a light pea green. If using for a soup, add a chopped tomato at the end for a pretty contrast.

QUICK BROWN STOCK

This stock is quicker—and less ideal—than the Brown Stock recipe because you don't start with browned bones. Instead, canned beef broth is cooked with vegetables and a little wine. If you have some bones, add them too, even if you don't have time to brown them properly in the conventional oven. They will contribute flavor and natural gelatins that help thicken the stock for sauces.

Preparation time: 15 minutes
Microwave time: 32–40 minutes
Yield: 4 cups

  1 small onion, peeled and quartered
  2 celery ribs with fresh yellow leaves
  2 medium-sized carrots
  1 small turnip, trimmed
  1 tablespoon butter
  4 cups canned beef broth
  1 cup chopped fresh or drained canned tomatoes
  ½ cup dry red wine
 10 peppercorns
  ¼ cup chopped fresh parsley
  1 bay leaf, crushed
  1 teaspoon fresh thyme *or* ¼ teaspoon dried
  4 pounds veal marrow bones (optional)

1. Use a food processor or knife to finely chop onion, celery, carrots, and turnip. Put vegetables in a 3-quart casserole. Add butter. MICROWAVE (high) 4–5 minutes, until softened, stirring after 1 minute.
2. Stir in rest of ingredients, including bones. Cover tightly. MICROWAVE (high) 18–20 minutes, until boiling, stirring after 10 minutes. MICROWAVE (medium) 10–15 minutes, until flavors develop. Strain. Taste. Because of the canned broth, salt will not be needed.

4

WHITE SAUCES

White sauce is to cooking what the forehand is to tennis. A good, solid white sauce marks you as a player in the game of cooking. And if you add to it a spice or slice of this or that, you'll create a winning game.

In French the word for white sauce is *béchamel* (BAY-shah-mel). But in either language, the ingredients are extremely simple: butter, flour, and milk, flavored with a little salt and pepper. The sauce is thick, creamy, and bland, one of the original comfort foods.

Although pure butter and whole milk produce the best texture, you can make an acceptable low-fat white sauce using margarine and skim milk. And you can even eliminate the margarine by thickening with cornstarch instead of water. Recipes are included for both of these low-fat white sauces.

Add grated Parmesan and Gruyère cheeses and you get a sharp Mornay sauce. A touch of tomato puree turns white sauce into a classic Aurore sauce. And tangy Dijon mustard quite disguises the sauce's plain origin.

As you read the recipes, note the various cooking techniques. For example, when onions are used, they are added with the butter to let them soften and develop flavor. However, minced garlic is added after the butter melts to avoid burning the garlic. In the Creamy Champagne sauce, the wine thins the sauce, so we start the basic white sauce with a little less milk.

PERSONAL CHART FOR CLASSIC WHITE SAUCE

Follow the descriptions for each step and write in the exact times needed for your microwave oven. You will have personalized instructions for a perfect, Classic White Sauce.

The first step is to make a roux, a cooked mixture of butter and flour. In conventional cooking, the mixture will burn if unattended for long. In the microwave oven, however, there is no single source of heat, so burning is unlikely.

To create a perfect white sauce in your microwave oven, start with:

> 2 **tablespoons butter**
> 2 **tablespoons flour**
> 1 **cup milk**
> ¼ **teaspoon salt**
> ⅛ **teaspoon freshly ground white or**
>   **black pepper**

	Instructions	Characteristics	Time Required (in minutes)
1.	Put butter in a 4-cup measure and MICROWAVE (high) until the butter is melted and very hot but still light yellow. (If the butter is right out of the refrigerator and you have a 600- to 700-watt oven, this will take about 2 minutes. If you let the butter get brown, the resulting sauce no longer will be a white sauce.)	Melted, light yellow	_____

Instructions	Characteristics	Time Required (in minutes)
2. Remove measure from oven. Thoroughly whisk in flour. MICROWAVE (high) uncovered until the mixture bubbles furiously. (In a 600- to 700-watt oven, this will take about 2 minutes. This is the most critical part of making white sauce. The flour needs to cook long enough to let the grains separate. This makes it capable of incorporating the milk and, ultimately, thickening the sauce. It also rids the sauce of a floury taste. If you don't cook the roux long enough, the specks of uncooked flour will mix with milk in the next step and create gluey lumps.)	Bubbling	_____
3. Remove measure from oven. Thoroughly whisk in milk. MICROWAVE (high) uncovered until bubbles that start at the edge of the sauce fill in and completely cover the top of the sauce. At this point, remove from oven and thoroughly whisk. (In a 600- to 700-watt oven this will take 2–2½ minutes if the milk is right out of the refrigerator. The mixture needs to reach this full boil to thicken. But you must stop and whisk to prevent lumps.)	Bubbles cover sauce	_____
4. Return sauce to oven and MICROWAVE (high) until sauce thickens. Thoroughly whisk in salt and pepper, preferably white pepper if you want to avoid black specks. (In a 600- to 700-watt oven, this will take about 2 minutes.)	Sauce thickens	_____

CLASSIC WHITE SAUCE

Here is a basic recipe for white sauce in a 600-to-700-watt microwave oven. For more detailed instructions, especially when using a lower wattage machine, please see Personal Chart for White Sauce (see pages 24–25).

Preparation time: 2 minutes
Microwave time: 8–8½ minutes
Yield: 1 cup

> 2 **tablespoons butter**
> 2 **tablespoons flour**
> 1 **cup milk**
> ¼ **teaspoon salt**
> ⅛ **teaspoon freshly ground white or**
> **black pepper**

1. Put butter in a 4-cup measure and MICROWAVE (high) about 2 minutes, until the butter is melted and very hot but still light yellow.
2. Remove measure from oven. Thoroughly whisk in flour. MICROWAVE (high) uncovered about 2 minutes, until the mixture bubbles furiously.
3. Remove measure from oven. Thoroughly whisk in milk. MICROWAVE (high) uncovered 2–2½ minutes, until bubbles that start at the edge of the sauce fill in and completely cover the top of the sauce. At this point, remove from oven and thoroughly whisk.
4. Return sauce to oven and MICROWAVE (high) about 2 minutes, until sauce thickens. Thoroughly whisk in salt and pepper, preferably white pepper if you want to avoid black specks.

TIP: For a thicker sauce, increase both flour and butter to 3 tablespoons each. For a thinner sauce, decrease flour and butter to 1 tablespoon each.

TIP: To make 2 cups medium-thick sauce, use 4 tablespoons butter, 4 tablespoons flour, and 2 cups milk. In Step 3, sauce will need 4–5 minutes to reach a boil.

TIP: *If sauce is too lumpy, put through a blender or food processor. However, the sauce then will be thinner.*

TIP: *If sauce is too thick, whisk in milk a tablespoon at a time. If sauce is too thin, MICROWAVE (high) to boil down and thicken; or stir in a tablespoon of butter.*

TIP: *Start with a 4-cup glass measure or similarly shaped bowl. This will give you plenty of room to boil and whisk one or two cups of sauce. A wide, flat dish is not as efficient because the sauce spreads out, making a small target for the microwaves.*

TIP: *Do use a whisk rather than a wooden spoon. It does a better job at fighting lumps.*

NO-BUTTER WHITE SAUCE

If you want to avoid butter and flour, you can make white sauce by simply thickening milk with cornstarch. I find that whole milk gives a better texture than skim milk.

Preparation time: 2 minutes
Microwave time: 6–8 minutes
Yield: 1 cup

> **1 cup milk, preferably whole**
> **1½ tablespoons cornstarch**
> **2 tablespoons water**

1. Put milk in a 6-cup measure. MICROWAVE (high) 3–4 minutes, until very hot.
2. In a cup, blend cornstarch and water until smooth. Stir into milk. MICRO-WAVE (high) 3–4 minutes, until thick, stirring after 1½ minutes, then every 30 seconds.

TIP: *The cornstarch version of white sauce tends to bubble up higher than those thickened with butter and flour. Take care not to burn yourself when this happens. A 6-cup measure—rather than a 4-cup measure—gives the sauce more room to rise safely.*

LOW-FAT WHITE SAUCE

You can make an acceptable white sauce using margarine instead of butter and skim milk instead of whole milk. Margarine melts faster and splatters more than butter, so I use less cooking time in Step 1. Also, the sauce is given an extra stir in Step 4 to avoid runovers.

Preparation time: 2 minutes
Microwave time: 7–7½ minutes
Yield: 1 cup

> **2 tablespoons margarine**
> **2 tablespoons flour**
> **1 cup skim milk**
> **¼ teaspoon salt**
> **⅛ teaspoon freshly ground white or**
> **black pepper**

1. Put margarine in a 4-cup measure and MICROWAVE (high) about 1 minute, until the margarine is melted and very hot but still light yellow.
2. Remove measure from oven. Thoroughly whisk in flour. MICROWAVE (high) uncovered about 2 minutes, until the mixture bubbles furiously.
3. Remove measure from oven. Thoroughly whisk in milk. MICROWAVE (high) uncovered about 2–2½ minutes, until bubbles that start at the edge of the sauce fill in and completely cover the top of the sauce. Remove from oven and thoroughly whisk.
4. Return sauce to oven and MICROWAVE (high) about 2 minutes, until sauce thickens, stirring twice. Thoroughly whisk in salt and pepper.

MORNAY

This very versatile cheese sauce suits macaroni and poached eggs as well as fish and chicken. The recipe starts with basic white sauce and is enriched with cheese. Some versions call for just Parmesan cheese, but I like this classic combination of Parmesan and Gruyère. Because the cheeses are light in color, Mornay sauce remains white. To get a browned look on a macaroni or light-colored fish dish, top with Mornay sauce, sprinkle with a little extra cheese, and brown under a broiler.

Preparation time: 5 minutes
Microwave time: 8 minutes
Yield: 1 cup

> 2 tablespoons butter
> 2 tablespoons flour
> 1 cup milk
> ¼ cup grated Parmesan cheese
> ¼ cup grated Swiss or Gruyère cheese
> ¼ teaspoon salt
> ⅛ teaspoon freshly ground white pepper
> Dash of cayenne pepper

1. Put butter in a 4-cup measure. MICROWAVE (high) 2 minutes, until melted and hot but still light yellow.
2. Remove from oven. Thoroughly whisk in flour. MICROWAVE (high) uncovered 2 minutes, until mixture furiously bubbles and foams but remains golden yellow—not brown.
3. Remove from oven. Thoroughly whisk in milk. MICROWAVE (high) uncovered 2–3 minutes, until whole top is covered with small bubbles.
4. Remove from oven. Thoroughly whisk. MICROWAVE (high) 2 minutes, until sauce thickens. Thoroughly whisk in Parmesan and Swiss or Gruyère cheeses. MICROWAVE (high) 2–3 minutes, until cheese melts. Thoroughly whisk. Taste for saltiness. Whisk in salt and both peppers. Taste again and adjust seasonings if necessary.

TIP: Cheese will melt better if it is finely grated.

TIP: Cheese typically contains salt, so note that the extra salt is added only after you have added the cheese and tasted the sauce.

GOAT CHEESE

A mild, fresh chevre, or goat, cheese such as Montrachet adds a special flavor to sauces. However, the extra cheese makes a typical white sauce quite thick. For a thinner version, start with a thinner white sauce, using 1 tablespoon each of flour and butter.

Preparation time: 5 minutes
Microwave time: 7-9 minutes
Yield: 1½ cups

> 1 tablespoon butter
> 1 tablespoon flour
> 1 cup milk
> ¼ teaspoon salt
> ⅛ teaspoon freshly ground white pepper
> ¾ cup fresh goat cheese

1. Put butter in a 4-cup measure. MICROWAVE (high) 1-2 minutes, until melted and hot but still light yellow.
2. Remove from oven. Thoroughly whisk in flour. MICROWAVE (high) uncovered 2 minutes, until mixture furiously bubbles and foams but remains golden yellow—not brown.
3. Remove from oven. Thoroughly whisk in milk. MICROWAVE (high) uncovered 2-3 minutes, until whole top is covered with small bubbles.
4. Remove from oven. Thoroughly whisk. MICROWAVE (high) 2 minutes, until sauce thickens. Thoroughly whisk in salt, pepper, and goat cheese.

BASIL CREAM

A handful of fresh basil adds color as well as a pleasant, mild taste to white sauce.
A touch of lemon intensifies the flavor.

Preparation time: 5 minutes
Microwave time: 8 minutes
Yield: 1 cup

> 2 tablespoons butter
> 2 tablespoons flour
> 1 cup milk
> 3 tablespoons finely chopped fresh basil
> 1 tablespoon fresh lemon juice
> ¼ teaspoon salt
> ⅛ teaspoon freshly ground black pepper

1. Put butter in a 4-cup measure. MICROWAVE (high) 2 minutes, until melted and hot but still light yellow.
2. Remove from oven. Thoroughly whisk in flour. MICROWAVE (high) uncovered 2 minutes, until mixture furiously bubbles and foams but still remains golden yellow—not brown.
3. Remove from oven. Thoroughly whisk in milk. MICROWAVE (high) uncovered 2–3 minutes, until whole top is covered with small bubbles.
4. Remove from oven. Thoroughly whisk. MICROWAVE (high) 2 minutes, until sauce thickens. Thoroughly whisk in basil, lemon juice, salt, and pepper.

TIP: A generous amount of fresh herbs is needed to overcome naturally bland white sauce. Do chop the fresh basil quite fine—or your sauce will look like creamed spinach.

AURORE

A couple of tablespoons of tomato paste add a touch of sweetness plus a pretty light-red color to basic white sauce. Serve Aurore sauce with eggs, poultry, fish, or pasta.

Preparation time: 5 minutes
Microwave time: 8 minutes
Yield: 1 cup

> **2 tablespoons butter**
> **2 tablespoons flour**
> **1 cup milk**
> **2 tablespoons tomato paste**
> **¼ teaspoon salt**
> **⅛ teaspoon freshly ground black pepper**

1. Put butter in a 4-cup measure. MICROWAVE (high) 2 minutes, until melted and hot but still light yellow.
2. Remove from oven. Thoroughly whisk in flour. MICROWAVE (high) uncovered 2 minutes, until mixture furiously bubbles and foams but remains golden yellow—not brown.
3. Remove from oven. Thoroughly whisk in milk. MICROWAVE (high) uncovered 2–3 minutes, until whole top is covered with small bubbles.
4. Remove from oven. Thoroughly whisk. MICROWAVE (high) 2 minutes, until sauce thickens. Thoroughly whisk in tomato paste, salt, and pepper.

HORSERADISH

This homemade, creamy-textured sauce teams well with corned beef or full-flavored fish. A little vinegar and dry mustard add extra punch to the horseradish, and a touch of sugar smoothes the taste.

Preparation time: 5 minutes
Microwave time: 8 minutes
Yield: 1 cup

> 2 tablespoons butter
> 2 tablespoons flour
> 1 cup milk
> 3 tablespoons prepared horseradish
> 1 tablespoon white vinegar
> 1 teaspoon dry mustard
> ½ teaspoon sugar
> ¼ teaspoon salt
> ⅛ teaspoon freshly ground black pepper

1. Put butter in a 4-cup measure. MICROWAVE (high) 2 minutes, until melted and hot but still light yellow.
2. Remove from oven. Thoroughly whisk in flour. MICROWAVE (high) uncovered 2 minutes, until mixture furiously bubbles and foams but still remains golden yellow—not brown.
3. Remove from oven. Thoroughly whisk in milk. MICROWAVE (high) uncovered 2–3 minutes, until whole top is covered with small bubbles.
4. Remove from oven. Thoroughly whisk. MICROWAVE (high) 2 minutes, until sauce thickens. Thoroughly whisk in horseradish, vinegar, mustard, sugar, salt, and pepper.

TIP: Prepared horseradish mellows after the jar has been opened and stored in the refrigerator. For a good sharp taste, start with a fresh jar. Or even better, substitute 1½ tablespoons of grated fresh horseradish.

CREAMY GARLIC

The pungent taste of garlic mellows when cooked with milk in this creamy sauce.

Preparation time: 5 minutes
Microwave time: 8 minutes
Yield: 1 cup

> **2 tablespoons butter**
> **1 tablespoon minced fresh garlic**
> **2 tablespoons flour**
> **1 cup milk**
> **¼ teaspoon salt**
> **⅛ teaspoon freshly ground black pepper**

1. Put butter in a 4-cup measure. MICROWAVE (high) 2 minutes, until melted and hot but still light yellow.
2. Remove from oven. Thoroughly whisk in garlic, then flour. MICROWAVE (high) uncovered 2 minutes, until mixture furiously bubbles and foams but remains golden yellow—not brown.
3. Remove from oven. Thoroughly whisk in milk. MICROWAVE (high) uncovered 2–3 minutes, until whole top is covered with small bubbles.
4. Remove from oven. Thoroughly whisk. MICROWAVE (high) 2 minutes, until sauce thickens. Thoroughly whisk in salt and pepper.

CURRY SAUCE

Curry adds a strong golden color as well as rich taste to creamy white sauce. Stir in chunks of cooked chicken or fish and serve over rice for a quick meal.

Preparation time: 5 minutes
Microwave time: 8 minutes
Yield: 1 cup

> 2 tablespoons butter
> ¼ cup minced onion
> 2 tablespoons flour
> 1 cup milk
> 2 bay leaves, broken in halves
> 2 teaspoons curry powder
> ¼ teaspoon salt
> ⅛ teaspoon freshly ground black pepper

1. Put butter and onion in a 4-cup measure. MICROWAVE (high) 2 minutes, until melted and hot but still light yellow.
2. Remove from oven. Thoroughly whisk in flour. MICROWAVE (high) uncovered 2 minutes, until mixture furiously bubbles and foams but remains golden yellow—not brown.
3. Remove from oven. Thoroughly whisk in milk and bay leaves. MICRO-WAVE (high) uncovered 2–3 minutes, until whole top is covered with small bubbles.
4. Remove from oven. Thoroughly whisk. MICROWAVE (high) 2 minutes, until sauce thickens. Whisk thoroughly. Remove bay leaves. Whisk in curry powder, salt, and pepper.

TIP: For a lower-calorie version, substitute margarine for the butter and skim milk for the whole milk.

CREAMY CHAMPAGNE

When I drink champagne I prefer it brut. But a sweeter version, such as demi-sec, gives a special flavor to this creamy sauce. The extra liquid thins the white sauce a little, making it a pleasant texture for a fish entree. To keep the medium thickness, use only ¾ cup milk.

Preparation time: 5 minutes
Microwave time: 8 minutes
Yield: 1 cup

> 2 **tablespoons butter**
> 2 **tablespoons flour**
> 1 **cup milk**
> ¼ **teaspoon salt**
> ⅛ **teaspoon freshly ground white pepper**
> ¼ **cup champagne**

1. Put butter in a 4-cup measure. MICROWAVE (high) 2 minutes, until melted and hot but still light yellow.
2. Remove from oven. Thoroughly whisk in flour. MICROWAVE (high) uncovered 2 minutes, until mixture furiously bubbles and foams but remains golden yellow—not brown.
3. Remove from oven. Thoroughly whisk in milk. MICROWAVE (high) uncovered 2–3 minutes, until whole top is covered with small bubbles.
4. Remove from oven. Thoroughly whisk. MICROWAVE (high) 2 minutes, until sauce thickens. Thoroughly whisk in salt, pepper, and champagne.

TIP: *Note that the thick texture of this sauce comes from using butter and flour to thicken milk—not from fat-rich cream.*

5

VELOUTES

Like white sauce, veloute starts with a roux of cooked butter and flour. However, broth or broth with milk or cream is added instead of milk. The resulting texture and taste is light and refined.

Restaurants that can afford the kitchen help keep a supply of rich veal stock to make luscious veloutes. But you can do very well at home with homemade chicken stock or good-quality canned chicken broth. Fish stock or canned clam broth create a light fish veloute for seafood dishes.

A good veloute has a creamy texture and is thick enough to "nappe," or coat, a spoon. I have included two basic recipes to get you these results.

Classic Veloute uses a combination of chicken broth and cream. It is faster to make and benefits from the rich taste of cream.

Low-Fat Veloute uses only chicken broth—no cream. To thicken the sauce, the broth is reduced, that is, cooked for a length of time until much of the liquid evaporates. By conventional techniques, it would take about 1 hour to reduce chicken stock to veloute. In my microwave method for Low-Fat Veloute, it takes 12–15 minutes. If you are trying to avoid the extra fat from cream, you may appreciate this method.

PERSONAL CHART FOR CLASSIC VELOUTE

Follow the descriptions for each step and write in the exact times needed for your microwave oven. You will have personalized instructions for a perfect veloute.

The first step is to make a roux. In conventional cooking the mixture will burn if unattended for long. In the microwave oven, however, there is no single source of heat, so burning is unlikely.

A 4-cup glass measure will give you plenty of room to boil and whisk one or two cups of sauce. A wide, flat dish is not as efficient because the sauce spreads out, making a small target for the microwaves.

To create a perfect veloute in your microwave oven, start with:

> **2 tablespoons butter**
> **2 tablespoons flour**
> **1 cup chicken broth or stock**
> **½ cup whipping cream**
> **¼ teaspoon salt**
> **⅛ teaspoon freshly ground white or black pepper**

Instructions	Characteristics	Time Required (in minutes)
1. Put butter in a 4-cup measure and MICROWAVE (high) until the butter is melted and very hot but still light yellow. (If the butter is right out of the refrigerator and you have a 600- to 700-watt oven, this will take about 2 minutes. If you let the butter get brown, the resulting sauce will have a brownish tinge.)	Melted, light yellow	_____

Instructions	Characteristics	Time Required (in minutes)
2. Remove measure from oven. Thoroughly whisk in flour. MICROWAVE (high) uncovered until the mixture bubbles furiously. (In a 600- to 700-watt oven, this will take about 2 minutes. This is the most critical part of making the veloute. The flour needs to cook long enough to let the grains separate. This makes it capable of incorporating the broth and, ultimately, thickening the sauce. It also rids the sauce of a floury taste. If you don't cook the roux long enough, the specks of uncooked flour will mix with broth in the next step and create gluey lumps.)	Bubbling	_____
3. Remove measure from oven. Thoroughly whisk in broth and cream. MICROWAVE (high) uncovered until bubbles that start at the edge of the sauce fill in and completely cover the top of the sauce. At this point, remove from oven and thoroughly whisk. (In a 600- to 700-watt oven, this will take 2–2½ minutes if the cream is right out of the refrigerator. The mixture needs to reach this full boil to thicken. But you must stop and whisk to prevent lumps.)	Bubbles cover sauce	_____
4. Return the sauce to oven and MICROWAVE (high) until sauce thickens. Thoroughly whisk in salt and pepper, preferably white pepper if you want to avoid black specks. (In a 600- to 700-watt oven, this will take about 2 minutes.)	Sauce thickens	_____

CLASSIC VELOUTE

This basic veloute starts with a roux of butter and flour, then uses chicken broth and cream to flavor and thicken the sauce; the cream makes the sauce extra smooth and rich. It is the quicker of the two basic veloutes in this book.

Preparation time: 5 minutes
Microwave time: 8–10 minutes
Yield: 1⅓ cups

> 2 tablespoons butter
> 2 tablespoons flour
> 1 cup chicken stock or broth
> ½ cup whipping cream
> ¼ teaspoon salt
> ⅛ teaspoon freshly ground white or
> black pepper

1. Put butter in a 4-cup measure. MICROWAVE (high) 2–3 minutes, until the butter melts and is very hot but still light yellow.
2. Remove measure from oven. Thoroughly whisk in flour. MICROWAVE (high) uncovered 2–3 minutes, until the mixture bubbles furiously.
3. Remove measure from oven. Thoroughly whisk in stock or broth and cream. MICROWAVE (high) uncovered 2–3 minutes, until bubbles that start at the edges of the sauce fill in and completely cover the top of the sauce. Thoroughly whisk.
4. Return sauce to oven and MICROWAVE (high) 2–3 minutes, until sauce thickens enough to coat a spoon. Thoroughly whisk. Taste. Add suggested amounts of salt and pepper or to taste.

TIP: Do use a whisk rather than a wooden spoon. It does a better job at fighting lumps.

TIP: For a truly classic veloute, stir in ¼ cup chopped mushroom stems when you add the stock and strain before serving.

LOW-FAT VELOUTE

This version of thick, creamy veloute is made without cream. The trick is to cook the chicken stock until the stock is reduced by half. When the stock is reduced, its texture will thicken and its flavor will intensify. Be sure to taste first before adding extra salt, especially if you are using canned broth.

Preparation time: 5 minutes
Microwave time: 16–20 minutes
Yield: ¾ cup

> 2 **tablespoons butter**
> 2 **tablespoons flour**
> 1½ **cups chicken stock or broth**
> ¼ **teaspoon salt**
> ⅛ **teaspoon freshly ground white or**
> **black pepper**

1. Put butter in a 4-cup measure. MICROWAVE (high) 2–3 minutes, until the butter melts and is very hot but still light yellow.
2. Remove measure from oven. Thoroughly whisk in flour. MICROWAVE (high) uncovered 2–3 minutes, until the mixture bubbles furiously.
3. Remove measure from oven. Thoroughly whisk in stock or broth. MICROWAVE (high) uncovered 3–4 minutes, until bubbles that start at the edges of the sauce fill in and completely cover the top of the sauce. Thoroughly whisk.
4. Return sauce to oven and MICROWAVE (high) 9–12 minutes, until sauce thickens enough to coat a spoon. Thoroughly whisk. Taste. Add suggested amounts of salt and pepper or to taste.

TIP: For an even lower-fat version, substitute 2 tablespoons margarine for the butter.

FISH VELOUTE

A mixture of onion, carrot, celery, and mushroom stems adds extra flavor and gives a light tan color to this light fish sauce. For a smooth sauce, strain before serving and present the cooked, minced vegetables as a side dish.

Preparation time: 20 minutes
Microwave time: 11–16 minutes
Yield: ¾ cup

> 2 tablespoons butter
> 2 tablespoons flour
> 2 tablespoons minced onion
> ¼ cup minced carrot
> ¼ cup minced celery
> ¼ cup minced mushroom stems
> 1 cup fish stock or bottled clam broth
> ⅛ teaspoon salt
> ⅛ teaspoon freshly ground white or
>   black pepper

1. Put butter in 4-cup measure. MICROWAVE (high) 2–3 minutes, until the butter melts and is very hot but still light yellow.
2. Remove measure from oven. Thoroughly whisk in flour. MICROWAVE (high) uncovered 2–3 minutes, until the mixture bubbles furiously.
3. Remove measure from oven. Whisk. Stir in onion, carrot, celery, and mushroom stems. MICROWAVE (high) 3–4 minutes, until soft.
4. Thoroughly whisk in stock or broth. MICROWAVE (high) uncovered 2–3 minutes, until bubbles that start at the edges of the sauce fill in and completely cover the top of the sauce. Thoroughly whisk.
5. Return sauce to oven and MICROWAVE (high) 2–3 minutes, until sauce thickens enough to coat a spoon. Thoroughly whisk. Strain if desired. Taste. Add suggested amounts of salt and pepper or to taste.

LEMON VELOUTE

This light, tangy sauce is delicious drizzled over fresh asparagus or peas. The lemon rind adds extra zest.

Preparation time: 5 minutes
Microwave time: 8–10 minutes
Yield: 1⅓ cups

> 2 **tablespoons butter**
> 2 **tablespoons flour**
> 1 **cup chicken stock or broth**
> ½ **cup whipping cream**
> 2 **teaspoons grated lemon rind**
> 1 **tablespoon fresh lemon juice**
> ¼ **teaspoon salt**
> ⅛ **teaspoon freshly ground white or black pepper**

1. Put butter in a 4-cup measure. MICROWAVE (high) 2-3 minutes, until the butter melts and is very hot but still light yellow.
2. Remove measure from oven. Thoroughly whisk in flour. MICROWAVE (high) uncovered 2–3 minutes, until the mixture bubbles furiously.
3. Remove measure from oven. Thoroughly whisk in stock or broth and cream. MICROWAVE (high) uncovered 2–3 minutes, until bubbles that start at the edges of the sauce fill in and completely cover the top of the sauce. Thoroughly whisk.
4. Return sauce to oven and MICROWAVE (high) 2–3 minutes, until sauce thickens enough to coat a spoon. Thoroughly whisk in lemon rind and lemon juice. Taste. Add suggested amounts of salt and pepper or to taste.

TIP: For a lower-calorie version, omit cream and increase broth to 1½ cups. Add an extra 7-8 minutes cooking time in the last step to reduce broth to a creamy texture. Be sure to taste before adding salt, because the reduction will intensify the saltiness of the broth.

MUSTARD VELOUTE

This creamy mustard sauce works well with roast beef. Use a smooth, rather than grainy-style, mustard, for a more elegant look.

Preparation time: 5 minutes
Microwave time: 8–10 minutes
Yield: 1⅓ cups

2 tablespoons butter
2 tablespoons flour
1 cup chicken stock or broth
½ cup whipping cream
2 tablespoons Dijon or smooth, country-style mustard *or* ½ teaspoon dry mustard
¼ teaspoon salt
⅛ teaspoon freshly ground white or black pepper

1. Put butter in a 4-cup measure. MICROWAVE (high) 2–3 minutes, until the butter melts and is very hot but still light yellow.
2. Remove measure from oven. Thoroughly whisk in flour. MICROWAVE (high) uncovered 2–3 minutes, until the mixture bubbles furiously.
3. Remove measure from oven. Thoroughly whisk in stock or broth and cream. MICROWAVE (high) uncovered 2–3 minutes, until bubbles that start at the edges of the sauce fill in and completely cover the top of the sauce. Thoroughly whisk.
4. Return sauce to oven and MICROWAVE (high) 2–3 minutes, until sauce thickens enough to coat a spoon. Thoroughly whisk in mustard. Taste. Add suggested amounts of salt and pepper or to taste.

TIP: For a lower-calorie version, see Tip for Lemon Veloute (see Index).

CAPER VELOUTE

Capers, the pelletlike buds of the caper bush, add a distinctive, pungent taste to this sauce, which marries beautifully with fish. Be sure to taste the sauce before adding salt because the pickled capers will have soaked in vinegar and salt.

Preparation time: 5 minutes
Microwave time: 8–10 minutes
Yield: 1⅓ cups

> 2 tablespoons butter
> 2 tablespoons flour
> 1 cup chicken stock or broth
> ½ cup whipping cream
> 2 tablespoons drained, coarsely chopped capers
> ¼ teaspoon salt
> ⅛ teaspoon freshly ground white or black pepper

1. Put butter in a 4-cup measure. MICROWAVE (high) 2–3 minutes, until the butter melts and is very hot but still light yellow.
2. Remove measure from oven. Thoroughly whisk in flour. MICROWAVE (high) uncovered 2–3 minutes, until the mixture bubbles furiously.
3. Remove measure from oven. Thoroughly whisk in stock or broth and cream. MICROWAVE (high) uncovered 2–3 minutes, until bubbles that start at the edges of the sauce fill in and completely cover the top of the sauce. Thoroughly whisk.
4. Return sauce to oven and MICROWAVE (high) 2–3 minutes, until sauce thickens enough to coat a spoon. Thoroughly whisk in capers. Taste. Add suggested amounts of salt and pepper or to taste.

TIP: For a lower-calorie version, see Tip for Lemon Veloute (see Index).

CREAM OF MUSHROOM

Canned cream of mushroom soup never tasted this good. To use this light-colored, creamy sauce as a soup, thin it with an extra cup of milk.

Preparation time: 15 minutes
Microwave time: 13–17 minutes
Yield: 2 cups

3 tablespoons butter
2 tablespoons flour
$\frac{1}{4}$ pound (1$\frac{1}{2}$ cups) cleaned, sliced mushrooms
2 teaspoons fresh lemon juice
1 cup chicken stock or broth
$\frac{1}{2}$ cup whipping cream
1 teaspoon minced fresh tarragon *or* $\frac{1}{4}$ teaspoon dried
$\frac{1}{8}$ teaspoon freshly ground black pepper
$\frac{1}{4}$ teaspoon salt

1. Put butter in a 6-cup measure or bowl with high sides. MICROWAVE (high) 2–3 minutes, until the butter melts and is very hot but still light yellow.
2. Remove measure from oven. Thoroughly whisk in flour. MICROWAVE (high) uncovered 2–3 minutes, until the mixture bubbles furiously.
3. Remove measure from oven. Thoroughly whisk. Stir in mushrooms and lemon juice. MICROWAVE (high) uncovered 3 minutes, until mushrooms are soft, stirring twice.
4. Stir in stock or broth and cream. MICROWAVE (high) uncovered 2–3 minutes, until bubbles that start at the edges of the sauce fill in and completely cover the top of the sauce. Thoroughly whisk.

5. Return sauce to oven and MICROWAVE (high) 4–5 minutes, until sauce thickens enough to coat a spoon, stirring twice. Thoroughly whisk in tarragon and pepper. Taste. Add suggested amount of salt or to taste.

TIP: Note that this recipe works best in a larger, 6-cup measure or bowl. You could use a 4-cup measure, but you will have to stop and stir an extra time or two in Step 5 to keep the sauce from running up the sides and overflowing.

6

BROWN SAUCES

Despite their rich color and flavor, brown sauces are not as calorie laden as many white sauces. This is because there is little fat added. The deep flavor comes from browning beef bones for a stock, simmering a wealth of vegetables, and reducing the sauce until thick.

Butter can be added at the end to slightly thicken and flavor the sauce. However, the butter should not be stirred in or it will lighten the color of the sauce. Just place the butter on top, and swirl the sauce a little until the butter melts.

As in any sauce, use good-quality wines, especially if the recipe calls for adding the wine at the end of the recipe.

Brown sauces can be stored covered in the refrigerator for up to a week. After about four days, they should be removed from the refrigerator, brought to a boil, cooled, and returned to the refrigerator. Leave any fats on top to help protect the sauce and skim off before serving.

CLASSIC BROWN SAUCE

Also known as Sauce Espagnole, brown sauce is one of the most respected standards of a good cook. Whether you make the sauce conventionally, on the stove, or with the help of a microwave oven, it is time consuming. A good stock makes a tremendous difference in taste. The sauce is covered while cooking only in Step 1 to help draw out vegetable juices and then in Step 3 to start the sauce cooking. Most of the time the sauce is cooked uncovered to reduce volume and intensify flavors. There is no salt in this recipe because brown sauce often is used as a base for other sauces. If the sauce is used as is, you may want to add a touch of salt and pepper just before serving.

Preparation time: 20 minutes
Microwave time: 48 minutes–1 hour
Yield: 1½ cups

> 2 slices bacon, diced
> ½ cup diced onion
> 1 cup diced carrot
> 1 cup diced celery
> 2 tablespoons butter
> 2 tablespoons flour
> 3 cups beef stock
> ⅓ cup dry red wine
> 1 cup chopped fresh or drained canned tomatoes
> ¼ cup chopped fresh parsley

1. Put bacon in a 3-quart casserole. MICROWAVE (high) 1–2 minutes, until cooked but not crisp. Drain fat. Add onion, carrot, and celery to casserole. Cover to help draw out juices. MICROWAVE (high) 5–6 minutes, until very soft.

2. Put butter in a 4-cup measure. MICROWAVE (high) 1–2 minutes, until melted and hot. Whisk in flour. MICROWAVE (high) 4–5 minutes, until flour is cooked through and mixture turns a rich brown color. Add 1 cup of the beef stock. MICROWAVE (high) uncovered 2–3 minutes, until bubbly.
3. Stir flour mixture and rest of ingredients into the casserole with the vegetables. MICROWAVE (high) 5–7 minutes, until just boiling. Remove cover. MICROWAVE (high) 30–35 minutes, until reduced by half or until sauce is about as thick as whipping cream. Strain. When cool, skim fat from top.

DEMI-GLACE

Demi-Glace, or half-glaze, is basically brown sauce that is reduced by half to a thick, intensely flavored sauce. Serve when you have guests for game or a special roast.

Preparation time: 10 minutes
Microwave time: 34–40 minutes
Yield: 1¼ cups

> ½ cup chopped mushroom stems
> ¼ cup dry sherry
> 1½ cups Classic Brown Sauce (see Index)
> 1½ cups good beef stock

Put mushroom stems and half of the sherry in a 2-quart casserole. MICRO-WAVE (high) 3–4 minutes to soften mushrooms and release juices. Stir in Brown Sauce and stock. MICROWAVE (high) uncovered, 30–35 minutes to reduce by half. Stir in rest of the sherry. MICROWAVE (high) 1 minute. Strain.

BROWN MUSHROOM

This rich-colored, versatile sauce pairs especially well with steak or meat loaf.

Preparation time: 10 minutes
Microwave time: 5–7 minutes
Yield: 1½ cups

$\frac{1}{2}$ **cup sliced mushrooms**
1 **tablespoon minced shallot**
1 **tablespoon butter**
1 **cup Classic Brown Sauce (see Index)**
1 **teaspoon fresh lemon juice**

1. Put mushrooms, shallot, and butter in a 4-cup measure. MICROWAVE (high) 2–3 minutes, until softened.
2. Stir in Brown Sauce. MICROWAVE (high) 3–4 minutes, until heated through. Stir in lemon juice.

TIP: If you don't have brown sauce, substitute 1 cup beef stock or canned beef broth. Make a slurry with 1 tablespoon cornstarch and 2 tablespoons water and stir into the stock or broth. MICROWAVE (high) 2–3 minutes, until thickened. Stir in lemon juice.

MADEIRA

A touch of Madeira wine makes a good beef sauce even more delicious.

Preparation time: 5 minutes
Microwave time: 6-9 minutes
Yield: 1¼ cups

> 1 tablespoon minced shallot
> 1 tablespoon butter
> ¼ cup Madeira wine
> 1 cup Classic Brown Sauce (see Index)

1. Put shallot and butter in a 4-cup measure. MICROWAVE (high) 2-3 minutes, until softened.
2. Stir in wine. MICROWAVE (high) 2-3 minutes, until reduced slightly. Stir in Brown Sauce. MICROWAVE (high) 2-3 minutes, until heated through.

SAUCE ROBERT

This piquant brown sauce variation, also known as sauce charcutière or pork butcher's sauce, typically is served with pork.

Preparation time: 5 minutes
Microwave time: 7–10 minutes
Yield: 1 cup

> 1 tablespoon minced shallot
> 1 tablespoon butter
> 2 tablespoons white wine vinegar
> 1 cup Classic Brown Sauce (see Index)
> 2 teaspoons Dijon mustard
> ¼ teaspoon sugar

1. Put shallot and butter in a 4-cup measure. MICROWAVE (high) 2–3 minutes, until softened. Stir in vinegar. MICROWAVE (high) 2–3 minutes, until vinegar has almost evaporated.
2. Stir in Brown Sauce. MICROWAVE (high) 3–4 minutes, until heated through. Stir in mustard and sugar.

7

HOLLANDAISE

There is a mystique about Hollandaise that scares many a cook. Fortunately, turning butter, eggs, and lemon juice into a golden, creamy sauce is an easy trick in the microwave. And it takes but 1 minute.

Hollandaise is an emulsified sauce. That is, two ingredients—such as oil and water—that don't normally mix are convinced to blend into a stable mixture.

The unwilling couple in a Hollandaise is butterfat and water. Emulsifying agents—here, lemon juice and egg yolk—coat the droplets of butterfat so that the fat won't stick together and instead mixes with the water. Also, the emulsifying agents reduce the surface tension of the water, reducing the water's instinct to reject oil.

Hollandaise breaks down if the sauce gets too hot or is overbeaten. The cure, as noted in the recipe Tips, is to add extra emulsifying agents, either milk, or eggs with dry mustard.

Once you have mastered the perfect Hollandaise, you can add a little tomato paste to make a Choron sauce, some orange juice and rind for a Maltaise, or a touch of tarragon, wine, and shallot for an aromatic Béarnaise.

PERSONAL CHART FOR HOLLANDAISE

Use this chart to help you record the exact times needed in your microwave oven to create perfect Hollandaise.

½ cup (1 stick) butter
3 large egg yolks
1½ tablespoons fresh lemon juice

Instructions	Characteristics	Time Required (in seconds)
1. Put butter in a 4-cup measure. MICROWAVE (high) until softened but not melted. (In a 600- to 700-watt oven, room-temperature butter will take about 20 seconds. Butter straight from the refrigerator may need up to a minute.)	Softened but not melted	_____
2. In a small bowl, mix egg yolks and lemon juice. Add to butter. MICROWAVE (high), whipping with a whisk every 15 seconds. Sauce is done when it is smooth and thick. (In a 600- to 700-watt oven, this will take about 1 minute. The butter will be lumpy after the first two whippings. After it has cooked the full time and the sauce is smooth and thick, stop working. Further cooking or whipping will cause the sauce to separate or curdle.)	Smooth and thick	_____

HOLLANDAISE

This simple recipe is almost foolproof in the microwave oven.

Preparation time: 2 minutes
Microwave time: 1 minute
Yield: 1 cup

> ½ **cup (1 stick) butter**
> 3 **large egg yolks**
> 1½ **tablespoons fresh lemon juice**

1. Put butter in a 4-cup measure. MICROWAVE (high) 20 seconds, until softened but not melted. (Butter straight from the cold refrigerator may need up to a minute.)
2. In a small bowl, mix egg yolks and lemon juice. Add to butter. MICRO-WAVE (high) 1 minute, whipping with whisk every 15 seconds. Sauce is done when it is smooth and thick.

TIP: The butter will be lumpy after the first two whippings. After it has cooked the full time and the sauce is smooth and thick, stop working. Further cooking or whipping will cause the sauce to separate or curdle.

TIP: If the sauce curdles, use one of these techniques:
- *Put 2 tablespoons milk in a 1-cup measure. MICROWAVE (high) 30 seconds, until boiling. Slowly whisk the milk into the curdled sauce until it is smooth again.*
- *Mix 1 egg yolk and a pinch of dry mustard in a 2-cup measure. Add about 2 tablespoons of the curdled sauce to the egg mixture and whisk. Add the mixture back to the curdled sauce and whisk until smooth.*

MOUSSELINE

It's hard not to eat large spoonfuls of this luscious-tasting sauce, which is basically Hollandaise with whipped cream folded in. Because it is so rich, you may want to reserve this sauce for special occasions and then use it sparingly—a few teaspoons on the tips of asparagus or a dab in the middle of a salmon steak.

Preparation time: 5 minutes
Microwave time: 1 minute
Yield: 1½ cups

> ½ cup whipped cream
> ½ cup (1 stick) butter
> 3 large egg yolks
> 1½ tablespoons fresh lemon juice

1. Keep whipped cream in refrigerator until ready to use.
2. Put butter in a 4-cup measure. MICROWAVE (high) 20 seconds, until softened but not melted. (Butter straight from the cold refrigerator may need up to a minute.)
3. In a small bowl, mix egg yolks and lemon juice. Add to butter. MICRO-WAVE (high) 1 minute, whipping with whisk every 15 seconds. Sauce should be smooth and thick.
4. Just before serving, fold in whipped cream (see Tip).

TIP: To fold, first gently spoon whipped cream on top of Hollandaise. Using a large spoon, start at the bottom of the sauce and gently spoon up, over, and through the whipped cream. Continue spooning until Hollandaise and whipped cream are partially mixed but whipped cream is still visible and fluffy.

MALTAISE

A little juice and rind from a fresh orange add sweetness and a faint blush of color to this classic variation of Hollandaise.

Preparation time: 5 minutes
Microwave time: 1 minute
Yield: 1 cup

> ½ cup (1 stick) butter
> 3 large egg yolks
> 1½ tablespoons fresh lemon juice
> 2 tablespoons fresh orange juice
> 1 tablespoon grated orange rind

1. Put butter in a 4-cup measure. MICROWAVE (high) 20 seconds, until softened but not melted. (Butter straight from the cold refrigerator may need up to a minute.)
2. In a small bowl, mix egg yolks and lemon juice. Add to butter. MICRO-WAVE (high) 1 minute, whipping with whisk every 15 seconds. Sauce should be smooth and thick. Stir in orange juice and rind.

BEARNAISE

A classic with beef tenderloin or steak. While the meat is on the grill, whip up this creamy, tarragon-flavored accompaniment in the microwave. The sauce is basically Hollandaise with a little less lemon juice, plus a touch of wine, tarragon, and shallot.

Preparation time: 5 minutes
Microwave time: 1 minute
Yield: 1 cup

> ½ cup (1 stick) butter
> 3 large egg yolks
> 1 tablespoon fresh lemon juice
> 2 tablespoons dry white wine
> 1 teaspoon minced shallot
> 2 tablespoons fresh tarragon *or*
>   1 teaspoon dried

1. Put butter in a 4-cup measure. MICROWAVE (high) 20 seconds, until softened but not melted. (Butter straight from the cold refrigerator may need up to a minute.)
2. In a small bowl, mix egg yolks, lemon juice, wine, shallot, and tarragon. Add to butter. MICROWAVE (high) 1 minute, whipping with whisk every 15 seconds. Sauce is done when it is smooth and thick.

CHORON

A little tomato paste turns Béarnaise into a classic Choron sauce, typically served with meat or chicken.

Preparation time: 5 minutes
Microwave time: 1 minute
Yield: 1 cup

½ cup (1 stick) butter
3 large egg yolks
1 tablespoon fresh lemon juice
2 tablespoons dry white wine
1 teaspoon minced shallot
2 tablespoons fresh tarragon *or*
   1 teaspoon dried
2 tablespoons tomato paste

1. Put butter in a 4-cup measure. MICROWAVE (high) 20 seconds, until softened but not melted. (Butter straight from the cold refrigerator may need up to a minute.)
2. In a small bowl, mix egg yolks, lemon juice, wine, shallot, and tarragon. Add to butter. MICROWAVE (high) 1 minute, whipping with whisk every 15 seconds. Sauce should be smooth and thick. Stir in tomato paste.

8

BUTTER SAUCES

Butter sauces are among the simplest accompaniments to make, and they find a home with food ranging from fresh asparagus to whole pike. Vary a favorite dish by experimenting with Garlic Butter, Basil Butter, or Beurre Blanc, one of the favorites in nouvelle cuisine.

Margarine substitutes fairly well for butter in the Meunière, Polonaise, Garlic, and Basil butters. But for best results, use pure, unsalted butter.

CLARIFIED BUTTER

Clarified Butter is what remains after you melt butter and skim away the foamy, white milk solids. What remains is a clear, oily liquid. It tastes like butter, but it is preferred in some recipes because it can be heated to a higher temperature than whole butter without burning.

Traditionally, Clarified Butter is served with steamed whole lobster. In India, cooks use ghee, a form of Clarified Butter that can be kept safely at room temperature.

Preparation time: 5 minutes
Microwave time: 2–3 minutes
Yield: ¾ cup

½ pound (2 sticks) butter

1. Put butter in a 2-cup measure. MICROWAVE (high) 2–3 minutes, until melted.
2. Line a sieve with cheesecloth and pour the butter through the cheesecloth and into a container. Repeat if necessary to remove all lumps. Clarified Butter can be stored in the refrigerator for several months.

TIP: Cheesecloth is an open-textured cotton fabric that was first used to wrap cheese. Look for it in specialty cookware stores. To wash, put the rinsed cheesecloth in a lingerie bag and throw in the washing machine with the towels.

TIP: If you don't have any cheesecloth, melt the butter and use a large spoon to skim off and discard most of the foamy, white solids. Let the butter stand for 3 minutes on the counter to allow the rest of the milk solids to settle to the bottom. Skim or carefully pour the clear, or clarified, butter into a container. Discard the remaining white solids.

BROWN BUTTER

Butter develops a lovely hazelnut color when cooked for several minutes in the microwave. Brown Butter traditionally is used with broccoli, asparagus, or brains.

Preparation time: 1 minute
Microwave time: 6–8 minutes
Yield: ½ cup

¾ cup Clarified Butter (see Index)

Put Clarified Butter in a 9-inch pie plate. Cover with waxed paper, tucking two ends under pie pan to keep butter from splattering. MICROWAVE (high) 6–8 minutes, until butter is light brown. Strain through cheesecloth if necessary to remove all solids.

BLACK BUTTER

The butter is not really black but a deep brown—the color of dark beer. Black Butter may be used for Brown Butter when you want a richer flavor.

Preparation time: 1 minute
Microwave time: 10–12 minutes
Yield: ½ cup

> ¾ **cup Clarified Butter (see Index)**
> 1 **teaspoon fresh lemon juice**

Put Clarified Butter in a 9-inch pie plate. Cover with waxed paper, tucking two ends under to hold firmly in place. MICROWAVE (high) 10–12 minutes, until butter is dark brown. Stir in lemon juice. Strain through cheesecloth if necessary to remove all solids.

TIP: Lemon juice may be replaced by white vinegar.

MEUNIERE

A common item on traditional French menus, Meunière is basically Brown Butter with lemon juice and parsley. Drizzle over fish or fresh vegetables.

Preparation time: 1 minute
Microwave time: 6–8 minutes
Yield: ½ cup

> ¾ cup Clarified Butter (see Index)
> 1 teaspoon lemon juice
> 1 tablespoon minced fresh parsley

Put Clarified Butter in a 9-inch pie plate. Cover with waxed paper, tucking two ends under to hold firmly in place. MICROWAVE (high) 6–8 minutes, until butter is light brown. Strain through cheesecloth if necessary to remove all solids. Stir in lemon juice and parsley.

GARLIC BUTTER

Instead of plain butter, try adding a touch of garlic to serve with fresh artichokes or shrimp.

Preparation time: 2 minutes
Microwave time: 1–2 minutes
Yield: ½ cup

> **2 teaspoons minced fresh garlic**
> **½ cup (1 stick) butter**

Put garlic and butter in a 2-cup measure. Cover with waxed paper, tucking two ends under to hold firmly in place. MICROWAVE (high) 1–2 minutes, until butter is melted and garlic is tender but not browned. Strain if desired to remove garlic pieces.

TIP: *To make a milder Shallot Butter, substitute two teaspoons minced fresh shallot for the garlic.*

BASIL BUTTER

Fresh basil is best, but dried will do in a pinch to flavor this simple butter sauce. Try it on pasta or zucchini.

Preparation time: 2 minutes
Microwave time: 1–2 minutes
Yield: ½ cup

> **½ cup (1 stick) butter**
> **¼ cup chopped fresh basil *or* 1 tablespoon dried**

Put butter in a 2-cup measure. Cover with waxed paper, tucking two ends under to hold firmly in place. MICROWAVE (high) 1–2 minutes, until butter is melted. Stir in basil.

POLONAISE

This sauce with browned and buttery bread crumbs is a classic over fresh asparagus stems. The recipe below is thin enough to pour; for a thicker sauce that clings more, increase bread crumbs to ½ cup.

Preparation time: 1 minute
Microwave time: 6–8 minutes
Yield: ½ cup

> ¾ **cup Clarified Butter (see Index)**
> 1 **teaspoon lemon juice**
> ⅓ **cup fine dry bread crumbs**

1. Put Clarified Butter in a 9-inch pie plate. Cover with waxed paper, tucking two ends under to hold firmly in place. MICROWAVE (high) 6–8 minutes, until butter is light brown. Strain through cheesecloth if necessary to remove all solids.
2. Stir in lemon juice and bread crumbs. MICROWAVE (high) 2–3 minutes.

SHRIMP BUTTER

Before discarding shrimp shells, use them to create this delicately flavored butter. Traditionally, Shrimp Butter is used as a flavoring in other sauces. However, a little dab makes a pleasant accompaniment atop mildly flavored fish.

Preparation time: 15 minutes
Microwave time: 6–9 minutes
Chilling time: 15 minutes
Yield: ⅓ cup

Shells from 1 pound shrimp
½ cup (1 stick) butter
2 tablespoons water

1. Wash and towel dry shrimp shells. Spread on a 9-inch pie plate. MICRO-WAVE (high) uncovered 2–3 minutes, until crisp and dry. Let stand on the counter to cool and allow water to evaporate. Process in a food processor or blender until finely chopped. You will have about 1¼ cups of shells. Set aside.
2. Put butter in a 4-cup measure. MICROWAVE (high) 1–2 minutes, until melted. Stir in chopped shells and water.
3. MICROWAVE (medium) 3–4 minutes. Do not let boil. Line a strainer with cheesecloth. Strain butter into a 2-quart bowl filled with about 2 cups of ice water. Use a spoon to squeeze shells well. Refrigerate bowl about 15 minutes, until butter rises to the top and hardens. Skim off the butter and transfer to a small covered bowl. Store in the refrigerator.

BEURRE BLANC

A popular sauce in France and the United States, Beurre Blanc, or white butter, is a simple combination of wine, vinegar, and shallot with butter. Try it with pike or mackerel.

Preparation time: 10 minutes
Microwave time: 3–4 minutes
Yield: ¾ cup

> **2 tablespoons dry white wine**
> **2 tablespoons white vinegar**
> **1 tablespoon minced shallot**
> **¾ cup (1½ sticks) butter, diced, room temperature**
> **Dash of salt**

1. Put wine, vinegar, and shallot in a 4-cup measure. MICROWAVE (high) 3–4 minutes, until liquid is reduced to about 1 tablespoon.
2. Add butter and salt gradually while whisking. Sauce should be creamy and foamy. Strain if desired to remove shallot.

TIP: If Beurre Blanc gets too hot, it gets oily; too cold, it turns into hard butter. It's best to make the sauce just before serving. To keep the sauce warm, store in an insulated bottle.

TIP: Add your personal touch to Beurre Blanc by adding ¼ teaspoon dried thyme or tarragon to the wine and vinegar mixture before cooking.

BEURRE ROUGE

Red wine vinegar gives a pink tone to Beurre Blanc. It goes well with asparagus and leeks.

Preparation time: 10 minutes
Microwave time: 3–4 minutes
Yield: ¾ cup

> 3 tablespoons red wine vinegar
> 1 tablespoon minced shallot
> ¾ cup (1½ sticks) butter, diced, room
>   temperature
> Dash of salt

1. Put vinegar and shallot in a 4-cup measure. MICROWAVE (high) 3–4 minutes, until liquid is reduced to about 1 tablespoon.
2. Add butter and salt gradually while whisking. Sauce should be creamy and foamy. Strain if desired to remove shallot.

9

WINE AND BEER SAUCES

Cooking with wine and beer is an excellent way to add extra flavor to sauces without adding extra fat. This is an especially useful trick in the microwave when food cooks so quickly that resulting juices can taste a little thin.

The rule of thumb is to cook with wine that you also would be happy to drink. In other words, shun so-called cooking wines featured in supermarkets and instead use a good-quality—though not necessarily expensive—wine. I've given some specific wine or beer recommendations in the recipes.

Alcohol cooks off as you heat wine, so you don't have to worry about overloading your dinner guests. For taste's sake, however, don't overload the sauce. The flavor of the food—not the wine—should be the predominant taste in the sauce.

WHITE WINE AND MUSHROOMS

This fine-tasting, low-fat sauce is so chunky with mushrooms that it almost passes as a side dish. The small amount of butter in the recipe isn't necessary to keep the vegetables from sticking, but it adds good flavor.

Preparation time: 15 minutes
Microwave time: 14-19 minutes
Yield: 2 cups

$\frac{1}{2}$

1 teaspoon butter
$\frac{1}{2}$ pound mushrooms, sliced thin
$\frac{1}{2}$ cup finely chopped onion
$\frac{1}{3}$ cup dry white wine, such as Chablis, chardonnay, or white burgundy
1 cup chicken stock or broth
$1\frac{1}{2}$ tablespoons cornstarch
2 tablespoons water
2 teaspoons fresh lemon juice
1 tablespoon fresh thyme *or* $\frac{1}{4}$ teaspoon dried
$\frac{1}{4}$ teaspoon salt
$\frac{1}{8}$ teaspoon freshly ground black pepper

1. Put butter, mushrooms, and onion in a 4-cup measure. MICROWAVE (high) 3-4 minutes, until vegetables are softened, stirring once.
2. Stir in wine and stock or broth. MICROWAVE (high) 10-12 minutes, until reduced to 2 cups.
3. In a cup, mix cornstarch with water and blend until a smooth paste. Stir into wine and mushroom mixture. MICROWAVE (high) 1-3 minutes until thickened. Stir in lemon juice, thyme, salt, and pepper.

MARCHAND DE VIN

A classic red-wine sauce, this pairs well with grilled steak or roasted meats. Note that extra salt is optional. The stock or broth will become more salty after it is reduced, so taste before seasoning.

Preparation time: 10 minutes
Microwave time: 17–22 minutes
Yield: 1 cup

1 tablespoon butter
2 tablespoons finely chopped shallot
$\frac{1}{3}$ cup dry red wine, such as Bordeaux or burgundy
1 cup beef stock or broth
1 tablespoon cornstarch
2 tablespoons water
1 tablespoon cognac
1 tablespoon fresh lemon juice
$\frac{1}{8}$ teaspoon salt (optional)
$\frac{1}{8}$ teaspoon freshly ground black pepper (optional)

1. Put butter and shallot in a 4-cup measure. MICROWAVE (high) 1–2 minutes, until softened but not brown.
2. Stir in red wine and stock or broth. MICROWAVE (high) 15–18 minutes, until reduced by half.
3. In a cup, mix cornstarch with water and blend until a smooth paste. Stir into wine mixture. MICROWAVE (high) 1–2 minutes, until thickened. Stir in cognac, lemon juice, and salt and pepper if desired.

SWEET DARK BEER

Just like wine, the type and quality of beer make a difference in a sauce. This recipe won't work well with a light beer—the taste will be too thin and bitter. My choice here is a good dark beer such as the German Hacker-Pschorr. Try this unusual sauce with green beans, cabbage, or smoked meats.

Preparation time: 10 minutes
Microwave time: 10-13 minutes
Yield: 1 cup

> 1 cup beef stock or broth
> 2 tablespoons unsulfured molasses
> 1 teaspoon prepared mustard
> 2 bay leaves, broken in halves
> 1 teaspoon fresh thyme *or* ¼ teaspoon dried
> 1½ tablespoons cornstarch
> 2 tablespoons water
> ½ cup dark beer
> 5-6 drops hot-pepper sauce

1. Put stock or broth, molasses, mustard, bay leaves, and thyme in a 4-cup measure. MICROWAVE (high) 8-10 minutes, until reduced to ¾ cup. Remove bay leaves.
2. Mix cornstarch and water in a small cup and blend until a smooth paste. Stir into broth mixture. Stir in beer and hot-pepper sauce. MICROWAVE (high) 2-3 minutes, until sauce is thick. Stir.

HOT SAKE

Technically a beer, sake is a high-alcohol, clear liquid made from fermented rice. In Japan it is served warm and sipped from what look like little porcelain egg cups. Its sweet taste can become bitter if cooked too long. Try this very simple dressing on a tossed lettuce and curly endive salad.

Preparation time: 1 minute
Microwave time: 40–50 seconds
Yield: ¼ cup

> ¼ **cup sake**
> 1 **tablespoon malt vinegar**

Put sake and vinegar in a 1-cup measure. MICROWAVE (high) 40–50 seconds, until quite warm.

MANGO-RUM

Thick with luscious mango, this sweet sauce—actually closer to a puree—provides a memorable touch to a duck or pork dinner. We like this sauce so much that we swirl the leftovers into rice.

Preparation time: 10 minutes
Microwave time: 10–13 minutes
Yield: 1⅓ cups

> 1 large, ripe mango
> 2 tablespoons butter
> ½ cup chicken stock or broth
> ¼ cup rum
> ⅛ teaspoon ground cinnamon
> 2 tablespoons fresh lime juice

1. Peel and seed mango; chop flesh into ½-inch pieces. Put chopped mango and butter in a 4-cup measure. MICROWAVE (high) 1–2 minutes, until butter is melted and fruit is softened.
2. Stir in stock or broth and rum. MICROWAVE (high) uncovered 9–11 minutes, until reduced and thickened, stirring twice. Stir in cinnamon and lime juice.

10

GRAVIES

Juices from lovely meat or chicken roasts can be coaxed into fine gravy within minutes in the microwave. And they don't have to be heavy and fattening.

Au Jus, the simplest accompaniment, is merely fat-free juices cooked down until slightly thickened. Apple Brandy–Cherry sauce is thick with fruit and a little cornstarch, instead of butter. Other gravies in this chapter typically use 2 tablespoons of fat to make 1 cup of thick gravy. Used in modest portions, these gravies complete the presentation of a dish.

If you're too rushed to make gravy the night you make the roast, pour all the juices and fat into a measuring cup and store in the refrigerator. The fat will rise to the top and help protect the juices for at least one week. When it's time for leftovers, bring out the saved juices and create a nicely herbed gravy.

AU JUS

Prime rib au jus (oh-zjew—it's a toughie) always makes a restaurant entree sound more intriguing—and expensive. But it is merely French for "in juice." You can create your own Au Jus in minutes from the juices of a roast that you have made in the microwave or conventional oven.

Preparation time: 2 minutes
Microwave time: 6–10 minutes
Yield: ¾ cup

1 cup cooking juices

1. Pour all juices and fat into a tall measure or heat-proof glass container. Let stand 5 minutes to allow fat to rise to the top, or refrigerate overnight to let fat become firm. Skim off and discard fat.
2. Pour 1 cup defatted juices into a 4-cup measure. MICROWAVE (high) uncovered 6–10 minutes, until juices have reduced to ¾ cup and thickened slightly.

PAN GRAVY

Homemade gravy over mashed potatoes is my favorite all-American pig-out food. It's a Sunday dinner special that should never go completely out of style. If you don't have enough pan juices, add stock or even a good-quality canned broth. Taste the finished gravy before you add salt or pepper.

Preparation time: 5 minutes
Microwave time: 9–13 minutes
Yield: 1 cup

> 2 tablespoons fat from roasting pan, or butter
> 2 tablespoons flour
> 1 cup pan juices, adding stock or canned broth if necessary
> **Salt**
> **Pepper**

1. Put fat and flour in a 4-cup measure. Stir until smooth. MICROWAVE (high) 5–7 minutes, until mixture turns light brown and loses its raw flour taste, stirring twice.
2. Stir in juices. MICROWAVE (high) 4–6 minutes, until gravy bubbles fast and thickens, stirring twice. Stir well. Add salt and pepper to taste.

TIP: *If starting with juices and fat that have been stored in the refrigerator, lift off fat and place in a 1-cup measure. MICROWAVE (high) 30 seconds, until fat melts. This makes the fat easier to measure. Gelatinlike juices can be spooned into a measuring cup without melting.*

TIP: *For Beef Pan Gravy, stir in 1 tablespoon tomato paste with the juices in Step 2. At the end, stir in ¼ teaspoon dried rosemary. This mahogany-colored gravy goes well with a pork roast too.*

TIP: *For Chicken Pan Gravy, at the end stir in 1 teaspoon fresh tarragon or ¼ teaspoon dried.*

APPLE BRANDY–CHERRY

Cherries, applesauce, and apple brandy are blended into a thick sauce that works well with duck, pork chops, or leftover chicken.

Preparation time: 10 minutes
Microwave time: 17–21 minutes
Yield: 2 cups

> 1 can (16 ounces) Bing cherries in thick syrup
> 1 cup defatted roast juices or beef stock or broth
> ½ cup applesauce
> 1 tablespoon cornstarch
> 2 tablespoons water
> 2 tablespoons calvados or apple brandy

1. Put cherries and ½ cup of the syrup in a food processor or blender and process until fine but not smooth. Put pureed cherries, roast juices, and applesauce in a 4-cup measure. MICROWAVE (high) uncovered 15–18 minutes, until reduced to about 2 cups and slightly thickened.
2. In a small bowl, mix cornstarch and water and blend until a smooth paste. Stir into cherry mixture. Stir in calvados or brandy. MICROWAVE (high) uncovered 2–3 minutes, until thickened.

TIP: To vary the sauce, substitute cherry-flavored Kirschwasser for the calvados or apple brandy.

SOUR CREAM GRAVY

Sour cream adds richness and a wonderful tang to gravy. Basic Pan Gravy is reduced to intensify flavor before the sour cream is added.

Preparation time: 5 minutes
Microwave time: 13–17 minutes
Yield: 1 cup

> 2 tablespoons fat from roasting pan, or butter
> 2 tablespoons flour
> 1 cup pan juices, adding stock or canned broth if necessary
> ¼ cup sour cream
> Salt
> Pepper

1. Put fat and flour in a 4-cup measure. Stir until smooth. MICROWAVE (high) 5–7 minutes, until mixture turns light brown and loses its raw flour taste, stirring twice.
2. Stir in juices, MICROWAVE (high) 8–10 minutes, until gravy bubbles fast, thickens, and reduces to ¾ cup, stirring twice. Stir well.
3. Stir in sour cream. Taste. Add salt and pepper to taste.

TIP: When reheating, do not allow Sour Cream Gravy to boil or the gravy will separate.

TIP: For extra zip, at the end stir in 2 teaspoons drained capers.

11

PASTA SAUCES

In our national quest to increase consumption of complex carbohydrates, it's wise to be armed with a variety of tempting sauces to moisten a plate of pasta.

Tomato sauces are a natural and the most common topping for pasta. I've included several varieties, from basic Fresh Tomato sauce and almost effortless No-Peel Tomato sauce to a chunky Mediterranean Olive version.

Then, to encourage a little more variety in meals, you'll find other toppings such as White Clam sauce, Lemon-Pecan sauce, or Creamy Red Pepper Puree.

Most of these pasta sauces are very easy to make, requiring uncomplicated techniques. Note that large bowls are used to make it easier to stir the sauce while cooking and that most of the pasta sauces are cooked uncovered to help the sauce thicken.

FRESH TOMATO

This simple Fresh Tomato sauce is ideal when garden-ripe tomatoes are at their peak. The tomatoes are cooked uncovered to let moisture evaporate and the sauce thicken.

Preparation time: 15 minutes
Microwave time: 15–18 minutes
Yield: 2 cups

> 2 **pounds fresh tomatoes, peeled, seeded, and chopped coarse**
> 1 **tablespoon olive oil**
> ½ **teaspoon salt**
> ⅛ **teaspoon pepper**

Put all ingredients in a 3-quart casserole. MICROWAVE (high) uncovered 15–18 minutes, until sauce thickens, stirring three times.

TIP: 2 pounds tomatoes = 8 small tomatoes = 3 cups chopped

TIP: To peel a fresh tomato, use a paring knife to cut out the stem. Make an X on that same bottom side. Plunge the tomato into rapidly boiling water for 20–30 seconds, then rinse under cold water. Use your fingers to pull the skin off the tomato, starting at the points of the X.

TIP: To seed a fresh tomato, cut the tomato in half horizontally. Hold tomato halves cut side down in palm of hands and gently squeeze out seeds over a bowl or the sink.

NO-PEEL TOMATO

Some cooks hesitate to make a fresh tomato sauce because they don't want to peel the tomatoes. (See Tip for Fresh Tomato sauce). You can skip that step if you puree the sauce in the food processor. The resulting sauce will be slightly chewy.

Preparation time: 10 minutes
Microwave time: 15–20 minutes
Yield: 2 cups

1 tablespoon olive oil
1 small onion, chopped fine
1 tablespoon minced garlic
2 pounds fresh tomatoes, quartered,
   stem ends removed
1/4 cup tomato paste
1 teaspoon minced fresh oregano *or*
   1/4 teaspoon dried
2 teaspoons minced fresh basil *or*
   1/2 teaspoon dried
1/2 teaspoon sugar
1/4 teaspoon salt
1/8 teaspoon freshly ground black pepper
1/4 teaspoon red pepper flakes

1. Put olive oil, onion, and garlic in a 3-quart casserole. MICROWAVE (high) 2 minutes, until softened.
2. Stir in tomatoes. MICROWAVE (high) uncovered 8–10 minutes, until tomatoes are very soft, stirring three times.
3. Puree tomato mixture in food processor. Return to casserole.
4. Stir in rest of ingredients. MICROWAVE (high) uncovered 5–8 minutes, until thickened.

TIP: 1/4 cup tomato paste = 1/3 of a 6-ounce can

ITALIAN MEAT

This chunky sauce, filled with meat and tomatoes, makes pasta a hearty meal.

Preparation time: 25 minutes
Microwave time: 20-26 minutes
Yield: 1 quart

  1 tablespoon olive oil
  1 small onion, minced
  1 teaspoon minced fresh garlic
  1 pound lean ground beef
  ½ teaspoon salt
  ⅛ teaspoon freshly ground black pepper
  2 pounds fresh tomatoes, skinned (see
    Tip for Fresh Tomato sauce), seeded,
    and chopped *or* 1 29-ounce can
    tomatoes, chopped, with juices
  ¼ cup tomato paste
  1 bay leaf, broken in half
  1 tablespoon chopped fresh basil *or*
    1 teaspoon dried
  1 tablespoon chopped fresh oregano *or*
    1 teaspoon dried
  ¼ teaspoon sugar
  2 tablespoons chopped fresh parsley

1. Put olive oil, onion, and garlic in a 3-quart casserole. MICROWAVE (high) 2-3 minutes, until softened.
2. Break beef into small pieces and add to olive oil mixture. Stir in salt and pepper. Cover with plastic wrap and vent one corner. MICROWAVE (high) 3-5 minutes, until meat is no longer pink, stirring twice. Drain.

3. Stir in rest of ingredients, except parsley. Cover with plastic wrap and vent one corner. MICROWAVE (high) 10-12 minutes, until sauce starts to thicken. Uncover. MICROWAVE (high) 5-6 minutes, until thickened. Remove bay leaf. Sprinkle with parsley just before serving.

TIP: Salt and pepper are added when the meat starts to cook to help give it flavor.

QUICK TOMATO

Good-quality canned tomatoes make better tomato sauce than fresh, pale winter tomatoes from the grocery.

Preparation time: 5 minutes
Microwave time: 15–18 minutes
Yield: 2 cups

> 1 **can (1 pound, 11 ounces) tomatoes**
>   **with juices**
> 1 **tablespoon olive oil**
> $\frac{1}{4}$ **teaspoon salt**
> $\frac{1}{8}$ **teaspoon pepper**

Coarsely chop tomatoes. Put all ingredients in a 3-quart casserole. MICRO-WAVE (high) uncovered 15-18 minutes, until sauce thickens, stirring three times.

TIP: Most canned tomatoes have added salt, so this recipe calls for less salt than recipes made with fresh tomatoes.

TIP: 1 can (1 pound, 11 ounces) = 3 cups tomatoes

MEDITERRANEAN OLIVE

Tomatoes serve as the base, but olives—both black and green—steal the show in this colorful sauce. Serve it with pasta or atop fish.

Preparation time: 20 minutes
Microwave time: 15–18 minutes
Yield: 2 cups

1	tablespoon olive oil
½	cup minced onion
1	tablespoon minced fresh garlic
½	cup dry white wine
1	cup tomato, peeled, seeded, and chopped coarse
¼	cup black olives, pitted and sliced
¼	cup green olives, pitted and sliced
½	teaspoon capers
½	cup bottled clam juice
¼	cup tomato paste
⅛	teaspoon red pepper flakes
1	tablespoon chopped fresh parsley

1. Put olive oil, onion, and garlic in a 2-quart casserole. MICROWAVE (high) 2–3 minutes, until softened.
2. Stir in rest of ingredients except for parsley. MICROWAVE (high) uncovered 13–15 minutes, until thickened, stirring twice. Sprinkle with parsley.

TIP: *Don't be tempted to pour in extra olive oil in Step 1. You don't need oil to prevent food from sticking in the microwave; the olive oil is for flavor. And you'll get plenty of extra flavor from the chopped olives.*

TIP: Note that no extra salt is added to this recipe. You'll get plenty from the tomatoes, olives, capers, and clam juice.

TIP: Working with a jar of green olives stuffed with pimiento? Just leave the pimiento in for extra flavor and color.

ALFREDO

Fettuccine Alfredo relies on this creamy, rich cheese sauce, which is very easy to make. The recipe provides ample sauce for 12 ounces, or four servings of fettuccine. The sauce will be slightly thin when you mix it into the fettuccine but will thicken within a couple of minutes as it is absorbed by the pasta.

Preparation time: 10 minutes
Microwave time: 7–9 minutes
Yield: 2 cups

> 1½ **cups half-and-half**
> 2 **eggs**
> ½ **cup grated Parmesan cheese**
> 2 **tablespoons butter**
> ¼ **teaspoon salt**
> ⅛ **teaspoon pepper**

1. Put half-and-half in a 2-quart casserole. MICROWAVE (high) 5–6 minutes, until simmering.
2. Meanwhile, beat eggs in a small bowl until frothy.
3. Add cheese, then beaten eggs, to half-and-half. MICROWAVE (medium) 2–3 minutes, until cheese melts. Stir well. Stir in butter, salt, and pepper.

TIP: Make the Alfredo sauce as the fettuccine is cooking. Mix together and serve with extra grated Parmesan cheese.

WHITE CLAM

This light sauce moistens pasta with tangy wine and clam flavors, and the clams add extra texture to the dish.

Preparation time: 15 minutes
Microwave time: 5–7 minutes
Yield: 2 cups

> 3 tablespoons olive oil
> ½ cup minced onion
> 2 teaspoons minced fresh garlic
> 1 tablespoon minced hot pepper, such as jalapeño
> ½ cup dry white wine
> 3 tablespoons minced fresh basil *or* 1 teaspoon dried
> 1 teaspoon chopped fresh oregano *or* ¼ teaspoon dried
> ⅓ cup fresh lemon juice
> 2 cans (10 ounces each) minced clams, drained
> 3 tablespoons finely chopped fresh parsley
> 1 teaspoon salt
> ¼ teaspoon freshly ground black pepper

1. Put olive oil, onion, garlic, and hot pepper in a 2-quart casserole. MICRO-WAVE (high) 2–3 minutes, until vegetables are soft.
2. Stir in wine, basil, oregano, and lemon juice. MICROWAVE (high) 2–3 minutes, until simmering.
3. Stir in clams. MICROWAVE 1 minute, until heated through. Stir in parsley, salt, and pepper.

TIP: Before mincing the hot pepper, discard the seeds and trim away the pithy core.

The veins, or core, and the adjacent seeds contain the most heat and can be an unpleasant surprise in a sauce.

TIP: *Choose a good-quality wine for this sauce—one you would be pleased to drink with dinner. The half cup is a substantial amount and the short cooking time isn't enough to disguise a poor-quality wine.*

HOT GARLIC-GINGER

The pain in this sauce is directly proportional to the amount of garlic, ginger, and hot chili peppers that you throw in. The suggested amount makes a pound of pasta mildly hot. Top with grated Parmesan cheese.

Preparation time: 5 minutes
Microwave time: 1 minute
Yield: ½ cup

> ½ **cup olive oil**
> 2 **tablespoons minced fresh garlic**
> 2 **quarter-sized slices fresh ginger**
> 2 **tablespoons minced hot chili peppers**

Mix all ingredients in a 2-cup measure. MICROWAVE (high) 1–2 minutes, until gently boiling. Let stand 5 minutes to allow vegetables to soften and the flavors to develop. Use a fork to remove and discard ginger pieces. Mix sauce into pasta.

TIP: *Be careful that you do not cook the oil so long that you fry the garlic. It will taste bitter.*

TIP: *Note that the fresh ginger slices are left in to flavor the oil, then removed to avoid chewy bits in the pasta.*

LEMON-PECAN

Moisture in this light sauce comes primarily from chicken stock or broth, which is cooked down to make it creamy. The sauce has little fat—only 2 tablespoons of butter. If left on pasta to cool, the pasta will absorb all the sauce and stick together. For this reason, serve it immediately on hot pasta, particularly rotini, which catches the nuts in its twists.

Preparation time: 10 minutes
Microwave time: 17–24 minutes
Yield: 1 cup

$\frac{1}{2}$ cup chopped pecans
2 tablespoons butter
2 tablespoons flour
$1\frac{1}{2}$ cups chicken stock or broth
1 tablespoon grated lemon rind
2 tablespoons fresh lemon juice
$\frac{1}{4}$ teaspoon salt
$\frac{1}{8}$ teaspoon freshly ground black pepper

1. Put pecans in a 1-cup measure. MICROWAVE (high) 2–3 minutes, until warm and flavors develop, stirring once. Set aside.
2. Put butter in a 4-cup measure. MICROWAVE (high) 2–3 minutes, until the butter melts and is very hot but still light yellow.
3. Remove measure from oven. Thoroughly whisk in flour. MICROWAVE (high) uncovered 2–3 minutes, until the mixture bubbles furiously.
4. Remove measure from oven. Thoroughly whisk in stock or broth. MICRO-WAVE (high) uncovered 2–3 minutes, until bubbles that start at the edges of the sauce fill in and completely cover the top of the sauce. Thoroughly whisk.

5. Return sauce to oven and MICROWAVE (high) 9–12 minutes, until sauce thickens enough to coat a spoon. Thoroughly whisk in lemon rind, lemon juice, and reserved pecans. Taste. Add suggested amounts of salt and pepper or to taste.

TIP: A 13¾-ounce can of chicken broth equals about 1⅔ cups broth. If you want, use all the broth in the can and just add an extra two minutes cooking time in Step 5.

CREAMY RED PEPPER PUREE

Redder than plain tomato sauce and sparked with contrasting nibs of black olives, this sauce intrigues as well as pleases. Red peppers and garlic are cooked in wine, which intensifies in flavor as it reduces in volume. The peppers and olives are chopped very fine in a food processor, then smoothed out with cream.

Preparation time: 15 minutes
Microwave time: 12–15 minutes
Yield: 2 cups

> **2** medium red bell peppers, cored, seeded, and chopped coarse
> **1** teaspoon minced fresh garlic
> **½** cup dry white wine
> **1** cup whole, pitted black olives
> **⅛** teaspoon cayenne pepper
> **⅛** teaspoon dried oregano
> **½** cup whipping cream
> **¼** teaspoon salt
> **⅛** teaspoon freshly ground black pepper

1. Put peppers, garlic, and wine in a 2-quart casserole. MICROWAVE (high) uncovered 10–12 minutes, until wine is reduced by half, stirring twice.
2. Stir in olives, cayenne pepper, and oregano. Puree in a food processor or blender until finely chopped but not smooth.
3. Stir in cream. MICROWAVE (high) 2–3 minutes, until heated through. Taste. Add suggested amounts of salt and pepper or to taste.

TIP: Mix with hot pasta and serve immediately, or mix, chill, and allow to reach room temperature before serving.

TIP: A 6-ounce can of black olives equals about 1½ cups olives. Save the extra ½ cup of olives to garnish the plate.

12

BARBECUE SAUCES

On a hot summer day, grill your entree outdoors and keep the kitchen cool by using the microwave to whip up the barbecue sauces. Some of the sauces here take as little as two minutes in the microwave oven.

And experiment. If you usually depend on an all-American tomato-based sauce, vary it with a touch of fragrant ginger, as in Buttery Ginger Barbecue. Or start with a bottle of exotic-tasting Dark Oyster Barbecue for a new accompaniment to fish. The recipes in this chapter are arranged in order from traditional to more unusual.

Because vegetables such as onions and garlic won't stick to the bowl when cooking in the microwave, little or no fat is needed in these recipes. When fats such as butter or olive oil are recommended, it is for flavor only, and you could eliminate them for a lower-fat version.

Note that the recipes call for cooking the sauce uncovered, at least for the end of the cooking. This allows moisture to evaporate so the sauce will thicken.

CLASSY KETCHUP BARBECUE

Thick, tangy ketchup is the perfect medium for making American barbecue sauce. If you want to get classy, you can add a good dose of dry red wine and some thyme, as we do here. Cook the sauce down to just less than 1 cup, until the sauce is thick enough to coat a spoon—or a big grilled steak.

Preparation time: 10 minutes
Microwave time: 14–18 minutes
Yield: almost 1 cup

> ½ cup finely chopped onion
> 1 teaspoon minced fresh garlic
> 1 teaspoon olive oil
> ⅓ cup ketchup
> ¾ cup dry red wine
> ¼ cup cider vinegar
> 1 tablespoon Worcestershire sauce
> ½ teaspoon dry mustard
> 1 tablespoon fresh thyme *or* 1 teaspoon
> dried
> ⅛ teaspoon freshly ground black pepper

1. Put onion, garlic, and olive oil in a 2-quart casserole. Cover. MICROWAVE (high) 2–3 minutes, until softened.
2. Stir in rest of ingredients. MICROWAVE (high) uncovered 12–15 minutes, until sauce thickens.

TEXAS SHARP BARBECUE

Plenty of Worcestershire sauce gives a good bite to this classic American barbecue sauce. Slather it generously on ribs or chicken.

Preparation time: 10 minutes
Microwave time: 10–13 minutes
Yield: 3½ cups

> 1 cup finely chopped onion
> 2 teaspoons minced fresh garlic
> 1⅓ cups cider vinegar
> 1¾ cups ketchup
> 1⅓ cups Worcestershire sauce
> 3 tablespoons unsulfured molasses
> ¼ cup fresh lemon juice
> 2 tablespoons dry mustard
> 1 bay leaf, crushed
> 2 teaspoons fresh oregano *or* ½ teaspoon dried
> ½ teaspoon freshly ground black pepper

1. Put onion, garlic, and about 3 tablespoons of the vinegar in a 2-quart casserole. MICROWAVE (high) 2–3 minutes, until vegetables are softened.
2. Stir in rest of ingredients. MICROWAVE (high) uncovered 8–10 minutes, until thickened.

SPICY MUSTARD BARBECUE

Anchovy paste is the secret ingredient in this nippy sauce. Use it to marinate chicken before cooking.

Preparation time: 10 minutes
Microwave time: 1–2 minutes
Yield: ½ cup

> ¼ cup minced onion
> 3 tablespoons olive oil
> ½ cup ketchup
> ¼ cup Dijon mustard
> 2 teaspoons anchovy paste

Put onion and olive oil in a 2-cup measure. MICROWAVE (high) 1–2 minutes, until softened. Stir in rest of ingredients.

BUTTERY GINGER BARBECUE

This butter-tinged, celery seed-speckled sauce pairs well with fish or ribs.

Preparation time: 10 minutes
Microwave time: 3–4 minutes
Yield: 1⅓ cups

2 tablespoons butter
½ teaspoon minced fresh garlic
¼ teaspoon finely chopped or grated
  fresh ginger
1 cup ketchup
2 tablespoons Worcestershire sauce
3 tablespoons fresh lemon juice
1 tablespoon brown sugar
1 teaspoon celery seeds
¼ teaspoon freshly ground black pepper

Put butter, garlic, and ginger in a 2-cup measure. MICROWAVE (high) 1–2 minutes, until vegetables are softened. Mix in rest of ingredients. MICRO-WAVE (high) uncovered 2 minutes, until thickened.

DARK OYSTER BARBECUE

Thick, bottled oyster sauce is thinned, sweetened, and spiced up a bit into a quick but memorable sauce. The flavors are intense, so use the sauce sparingly on fish or ribs.

Preparation time: 10 minutes
Microwave time: 2–3 minutes
Yield: ¼ cup

- ½ teaspoon minced fresh garlic
- ½ teaspoon minced fresh ginger
- ¼ cup bottled oyster sauce
- 2 tablespoons water
- 1 tablespoon fresh lemon juice
- 2 teaspoons sugar
- ⅛ teaspoon dried red pepper flakes

Put all ingredients in a 2-cup measure. MICROWAVE (high) 2–3 minutes, until garlic and ginger are softened. Stir well.

13

VEGETABLE AND SALAD DRESSINGS

When you're contemplating a new way to present a favorite salad or vegetable, consider drizzling the dish with a warm dressing, something as comforting as Sweet Sesame Vinaigrette or as upscale as Wild Mushroom dressing.

Most of the dressings presented here are oil-and-vinegar based, rather than mayonnaise based, which makes them easy to heat without the worry of breaking down the sauce. They also save calories, because you need less dressing to coat a salad.

Armchair cooks thumbing through these recipes will find some useful microwave techniques for "toasting" seeds or reconstituting dried mushrooms.

The dressings in this chapter may be the most useful sauces in the book, because they serve both meats and vegetables, warm or cold. Use the Suggested Food and Sauce Pairings list at the end of the book for serving ideas.

SWEET SESAME VINAIGRETTE

My Dallas-raised niece Missy Franklin introduced me to a honey-sweetened sesame dressing that she tossed with lettuce salad, then topped with grated longhorn cheddar cheese. The microwave oven makes it easy to "toast" the sesame seeds without worrying about burning them.

Preparation time: 5 minutes
Microwave time: 3–5 minutes
Yield: ¾ cup

2 tablespoons sesame seeds
1 teaspoon minced fresh garlic
3 tablespoons white wine vinegar
⅛ teaspoon red pepper flakes
⅛ teaspoon dried oregano
¼ teaspoon salt
⅛ teaspoon freshly ground black pepper
½ cup vegetable oil
¼ cup honey

1. Put sesame seeds on a small plate and shake to spread them. MICROWAVE (high) uncovered 2–3 minutes, until well heated. Set aside.
2. Put garlic, vinegar, red pepper flakes, oregano, salt, and pepper in a 4-cup measure. MICROWAVE (high) 1–2 minutes, until garlic and dried spices are softened. Whisk in oil and honey. Add sesame seeds.

VEGETABLE VINAIGRETTE

This colorful dressing adds extra, healthy vegetables to a salad or cold meat platter.

Preparation time: 15 minutes
Microwave time: 2–3 minutes
Yield: 1¼ cups

1 teaspoon minced fresh garlic
¼ cup diced green pepper
¼ cup diced sweet red pepper
½ cup peeled, diced cucumber
2 tablespoons lemon juice
2 tablespoons cider vinegar
1 tablespoon sugar
1 tablespoon Dijon-style mustard
½ teaspoon salt
⅛ teaspoon freshly ground black pepper
½ cup vegetable oil
1 tablespoon coarsely chopped capers

1. Put garlic, green pepper, red pepper, and cucumber in a 4-cup measure. MICROWAVE (high) 2–3 minutes, until vegetables are just softened, stirring once.
2. In a small bowl, whisk lemon juice, vinegar, sugar, mustard, salt, and pepper. Whisk in oil. Stir in capers. Add mixture to vegetables.

TIP: Capers add distinct flavor and tang, but if you don't like them, you can substitute a tablespoon of vinegar or chopped pickle.

HOT GERMAN

Pour this zesty dressing over still-warm potatoes or a platter of julienned carrots.

Preparation time: 10 minutes
Microwave time: 5-6 minutes
Yield: ½ cup

> 4 strips bacon, diced
> 2 tablespoons minced shallot
> 2 tablespoons apple juice
> 3 tablespoons cider vinegar
> 1 teaspoon dry mustard
> 1 teaspoon salt
> 1 egg, well beaten

1. Put bacon and shallot in a 4-cup measure. MICROWAVE (high) 4-5 minutes, until bacon is cooked, stirring once. Stir in apple juice, vinegar, mustard, and salt. MICROWAVE (high) 1 minute, until blended.
2. Beat a teaspoon of hot bacon mixture into egg. Beat egg into hot marinade until well mixed.

WARM ANCHOVY

This pleasantly pungent sauce is wonderful drizzled over fresh tomato slices.

Preparation time: 10 minutes
Microwave time: 1–1½ minutes
Yield: ⅓ cup

> 3 anchovy fillets, chopped coarse
> 1 teaspoon minced fresh garlic
> 2 tablespoons fresh lemon juice
> ⅛ teaspoon salt
> ⅛ teaspoon freshly ground black pepper
> 4 tablespoons olive oil
> 2 tablespoons minced fresh parsley

Put anchovies and garlic in a 2-cup measure. Use a fork to mash. Mixture will be lumpy, but it will smooth out after it has cooked. Stir in lemon juice, salt, and pepper. MICROWAVE (high) 1–1½ minutes. Whisk in oil and parsley until smooth.

WILD MUSHROOM

Dried porcini mushrooms, called cèpes *in France, add a rich, woodsy flavor to this red pepper–flecked dressing. It is elegant drizzled over a cold fish salad or a plate of Belgian endive and sliced button mushrooms.*

Preparation time: 15 minutes
Soaking time: 10 minutes
Microwave time: 2–3 minutes
Yield: 1 cup

> **4 tablespoons (½ ounce) dried porcini mushrooms**
> **½ cup red wine vinegar**
> **¼ cup diced sweet red pepper**
> **1 small onion, sliced thin**
> **½ cup olive oil, preferably extra virgin**
> **1 tablespoon chopped fresh tarragon *or***
> **½ teaspoon dried**
> **¼ teaspoon salt**
> **⅛ teaspoon freshly ground black pepper**

1. Put mushrooms and vinegar in a 1-cup measure. Cover with plastic wrap. MICROWAVE (high) about 1 minute, until boiling. Let stand, covered, 10 minutes.
2. Meanwhile, put red pepper, onion, and olive oil in a 4-cup measure. MICROWAVE (high) 1–2 minutes, until softened.
3. Drain mushrooms through water-soaked cheesecloth or a coffee filter, reserving liquid. Rinse mushrooms briefly under cold running water to get rid of any grit. Trim and discard tough ends from mushrooms; chop mushrooms.

4. Add chopped mushrooms, reserved liquid, tarragon, salt, and pepper to red pepper mixture. Whisk well.

TIP: *Look for dried porcini mushrooms in Italian or specialty food stores. Dried shiitake mushrooms, found in Oriental specialty stores, can be substituted.*

SOUR AND SWEET

More tart than sweet, this thick sauce is an unusual enticement drizzled over fresh corn. Or use it as a dip for crisp egg rolls.

Preparation time: 10 minutes
Microwave time: 1-2 minutes
Yield: ¾ cup

> 1 **tablespoon cornstarch**
> 2 **tablespoons water**
> ⅓ **cup cider vinegar**
> 1 **tablespoon soy sauce**
> ¼ **cup apricot jam**
> 2 **tablespoons ketchup**
> 2 **tablespoons brown sugar**
> 1 **teaspoon grated lemon rind**

Put cornstarch and water in a 4-cup measure and stir until well blended. Add remaining ingredients. MICROWAVE (high) 1-2 minutes, until thick.

14

CONDIMENTS

Homemade extras such as Hot Salsa or Mango Chutney can add excitement to an otherwise lackluster meal or plate of leftovers.

Most of the recipes here are low-fat, sweetened or spiced fruit. It's the surprises that make them special: a little orange and lemon in the cranberry sauce, a touch of calvados in the applesauce.

The microwave oven's part is pretty fast, typically 5–10 minutes for each recipe. But because the ingredients are fresh, you will need another 10–20 minutes to peel and chop them. One solution to the time crunch is to plan ahead and make at least part of the condiment the day before. Or while you make the entree, hand the condiment recipe and ingredients to an eager kitchen assistant.

NORMANDY APPLE

A couple of apples can be turned into fresh applesauce after just 10 minutes in the microwave. This version is enhanced with calvados, an apple brandy from Normandy, France. Serve it warm with pork or chicken.

Preparation time: 10 minutes
Microwave time: 8–10 minutes
Yield: 1 cup

1 **pound (2–3) tart apples (Granny Smith or McIntosh are good)**
2 **tablespoons calvados or other brandy**
2 **tablespoons water**
¼ **teaspoon ground cinnamon**
1 **teaspoon sugar**

Peel, core, and thinly slice apples. Put apples, calvados, and water in a 2-quart casserole. Cover. MICROWAVE (high) 8–10 minutes, until fruit is tender, stirring once. Puree in a food processor if desired. Stir in cinnamon and sugar.

TIP: *To serve as a dessert, increase sugar to 1 tablespoon.*

APPLE-ONION

Late May through July, when sweet Vidalia onions from Georgia are in season, this tart sauce is a special treat, especially with pork.

Preparation time: 20 minutes
Microwave time: 12–14 minutes
Yield: 2–3 cups

> 2 pounds (4 large) tart apples (Granny Smith are good), peeled, cored, and sliced
> 1 medium onion, minced
> ¼ cup water
> 1 tablespoon fresh lemon juice
> 2 tablespoons sugar

Put all ingredients in a 2-quart casserole. Cover. MICROWAVE (high) 12–14 minutes, until very tender, stirring three times. Serve as is, chunky style, or puree in a blender or food processor.

LEMON-ORANGE CRANBERRY

Fresh orange and lemon juices add an individual touch to homemade cranberry sauce. Serve it with turkey, of course, or everyday roast chicken or pork chops.

Preparation time: 5 minutes
Microwave time: 5–7 minutes
Yield: 2 cups

> 2 cups (10 ounces) fresh or frozen cranberries
> 2 tablespoons grated, minced orange rind
> ¼ cup fresh orange juice
> 1 tablespoon grated, minced lemon rind
> 2 tablespoons fresh lemon juice
> ¾ cup sugar

Mix all ingredients in a 2-quart casserole. Cover with waxed paper. MICRO-WAVE (high) 5–7 minutes, until cranberries pop open and sauce thickens, stirring twice.

HOT SALSA

Small, tart tomatillos make a great salsa that you can use to top baked potatoes or serve with tortilla chips. Serve warm or at room temperature.

Preparation time: 15 minutes
Microwave time: 5 minutes
Yield: 2 cups

1	tablespoon seeded, minced chili pepper
½	cup onion, chopped fine
1	teaspoon minced garlic
2	tablespoons vegetable oil
10-12	tomatillos, paperlike husks removed and chopped fine
2	tablespoons chopped fresh coriander (cilantro)

1. Put pepper, onion, garlic, and oil in a 2-quart casserole. MICROWAVE (high) 2 minutes, until softened, stirring once.
2. Stir in tomatillos. MICROWAVE (high) uncovered 2–3 minutes, until tomatillos just start to release juice. Do not overcook or you will lose both texture and tartness. Stir in coriander.

TIP: Italian plum tomatoes and a tablespoon of lemon juice can be substituted for the tomatillos.

MANGO CHUTNEY

This thick, sweet chutney is a colorful addition to a pork or duck dinner. It also serves well as a snack with thin crackers.

Preparation time: 20 minutes
Microwave time: 8–10 minutes
Yield: 2 cups

    2 ripe mangos
    ¼ cup minced onion
    1 teaspoon minced fresh garlic
    2 teaspoons minced fresh ginger
    ½ cup lightly packed brown sugar
    1 small tomato, peeled, seeded, and
      chopped fine
    ½ cup walnuts, chopped fine
    1 teaspoon mustard seeds
    ½ teaspoon cinnamon
    ⅛ teaspoon ground cloves
    ⅛ teaspoon cayenne pepper
    2 tablespoons fresh lime juice

1. Peel mango, remove seed, and finely chop remaining flesh. Mix with all other ingredients except lime juice in a 3-quart casserole. Cover with waxed paper. MICROWAVE (high) 2–3 minutes, until quite hot. Stir.
2. MICROWAVE (high) uncovered 5–7 minutes, until fruit is soft. Stir in lime juice.

15

DESSERT SAUCES

One of the surest ways to fall in love with a new microwave oven is to make a batch of homemade dessert sauces. The results—from healthful Fresh Raspberry sauce to decadent Rum Hot Fudge—are spectacular.

And the sauces are so easy to make. Most of the recipes here need only 10 minutes to prepare and 5 minutes or less to cook in the microwave. All use a 4-cup glass measure, which is handy for pouring the sauces and is very easy to clean in the dishwasher.

Enjoy the sauces over ice cream or for sweet fondues into which you dip pieces of cake or fruit.

FRESH RASPBERRY

Fresh raspberries are warmed in the microwave just until they soften into a thick sauce—perfect over vanilla ice cream. Very simple. Very good.

Preparation time: 2 minutes
Microwave time: 2–3 minutes
Yield: 1 cup

> **1 pint (2 cups) fresh raspberries**
> **1 tablespoon sugar**
> **¼ teaspoon vanilla**

Put raspberries and sugar in a 4-cup measure. Cover with plastic wrap. MICROWAVE (high) 2–3 minutes, until soft, stirring once. Add vanilla and stir to mix well but not too smooth. Chunks of raspberry give the sauce that nice fresh look.

CINNAMON-PEACH

This old-fashioned peach topping is a good family pleaser. For a grown-up variation, add 2 tablespoons cognac.

Preparation time: 10 minutes
Microwave time: 3–4 minutes
Yield: 1 cup

> **2 cups fresh ripe peaches, skinned,
> pitted, and chopped coarse**
> **2 tablespoons sugar**
> **⅛ teaspoon cinnamon**
> **¼ cup water**
> **2 tablespoons cognac (optional)**

Mix all ingredients in a 4-cup measure. Cover tightly. MICROWAVE (high) 3–4 minutes, until soft, stirring once.

CHUNKY CHERRY-NUT

When one cherry atop a sundae just isn't enough, try this thick mixture of chopped fresh Bing cherries, walnuts, and orange rind. Pour lavishly over ice cream in a tulip-shaped dish—and top with one more whole cherry, on a stem!

Preparation time: 10 minutes
Microwave time: 7–9 minutes
Yield: 1 cup

> **2 cups fresh Bing cherries**
> **1 tablespoon finely chopped orange rind**
> **2 tablespoons cherry-flavored liqueur**
> **3 tablespoons water**
> **2 teaspoons sugar**
> **¼ cup coarsely chopped walnuts**

1. Put cherries in a 4-cup measure. MICROWAVE (high) 3–4 minutes, until the cherries start to split. Let stand about 5 minutes to allow cherries to cool for easier handling. Remove and discard pits, saving any juices. Coarsely chop cherries.
2. Put cherries and juices back in the 4-cup measure. Add rest of ingredients except walnuts. Cover tightly with plastic wrap. MICROWAVE (high) 4–5 minutes, until fruit is soft, stirring twice. Stir in walnuts.

TIP: Note that a quick stint in the microwave softens fresh, whole cherries enough to make them easy to pit.

TIP: Brandy or just water can be substituted for the cherry liqueur.

BUTTERSCOTCH

Butterscotch has always seemed a bit magical to me, a distinctly new flavor created from butter, cream, and brown sugar, or sometimes molasses. This version is elegantly thin enough to serve under poached pears.

Preparation time: 5 minutes
Microwave time: 3–5 minutes
Yield: 1 cup

> ½ **cup butter**
> **1 cup dark brown sugar**
> ½ **cup half-and-half**
> ½ **teaspoon vanilla**

1. Put butter and brown sugar in a 4-cup measure. MICROWAVE (high) 2–3 minutes, until butter is melted and hot. Stir well.
2. Add half-and-half and vanilla. MICROWAVE (high) 1–2 minutes, until just before boiling, stirring after 1 minute. Stir well.

TIP: For a thicker, richer sauce, substitute cream for the half-and-half.

HONEY HOT FUDGE

Honey adds a distinct bite to this creamy-rich fudge sauce, wonderful over vanilla or butter pecan ice cream. The sauce is thin enough when warm to glaze a cake or the bottom of a dessert plate. It thickens over ice cream.

Preparation time: 10 minutes
Microwave time: 4–5 minutes
Yield: 2¾ cups

- ½ cup honey
- 1 cup confectioners' sugar
- ½ cup unsweetened cocoa
- 3 ounces unsweetened chocolate
- ½ cup (1 stick) butter, cut up
- 1 cup whipping cream
- 1 teaspoon vanilla

1. Put honey, sugar, cocoa, chocolate, and butter in a 4-quart measure. MICROWAVE (medium) 4–5 minutes, until chocolate and butter are melted, using a plastic spoon to stir well after 2 minutes, then every minute. Mixture will be thick and sticky.
2. Use a metal whisk to slowly whisk in cream 2–3 minutes until mixture is smooth, scraping bottom with a spoon if necessary. Whisk in vanilla.

TIP: Don't use a wooden spoon to stir chocolate. Moisture from the wood may tighten the chocolate and prevent it from melting evenly. Also, your wooden spoon will darken.

TIP: To reheat, cook on medium power 1–2 minutes, checking and stirring every 30 seconds.

RUM HOT FUDGE

This fabulous sauce is rich with butter and cream and is generously spiked with rum, an ideal topping for thin dessert crepes. If you're going to indulge, this is the way to go. (See Honey Hot Fudge Tips for cooking with chocolate.)

Preparation time: 10 minutes
Microwave time: 4–5 minutes
Yield: 2⅓ cups

> 1¾ cups confectioners' sugar
> ½ cup unsweetened cocoa
> 3 ounces unsweetened chocolate
> ½ cup (1 stick) butter, cut up
> 1 cup whipping cream
> 1 teaspoon vanilla
> ¼ cup rum

1. Put sugar, cocoa, chocolate, and butter in a 4-cup measure. MICROWAVE (medium) 4–5 minutes, until chocolate and butter are melted, using a plastic spoon to stir well after 2 minutes, then every minute. Mixture will be thick and sticky.
2. Use metal whisk to slowly whisk in cream 2–3 minutes, until mixture is smooth, scraping bottom with a spoon if necessary. Whisk in vanilla and rum.

SUGGESTED
FOOD AND SAUCE PAIRINGS

MEATS
Beef

Au Jus
Béarnaise
Beurre Rouge
Brown Mushroom
Caper Veloute
Choron
Classic Brown Sauce
Classy Ketchup Barbecue
Cream of Mushroom
Creamy Garlic
Dark Oyster Barbecue
Demi-Glace

Garlic Butter
Horseradish
Hot Garlic-Ginger
Hot Salsa
Madeira
Marchand de Vin
Mustard Veloute
Pan Gravy
Sour Cream Gravy
Sweet Sesame Vinaigrette
Texas Sharp Barbecue
Wild Mushroom

Ham, Tongue

Creamy Garlic
Horseradish
Hot German
Lemon-Pecan
Mustard Veloute

Normandy Apple
Sauce Robert
Spicy Mustard Barbecue
Sweet Dark Beer
Vegetable Vinaigrette

Hamburger

Brown Mushroom
Caper Veloute
Cream of Mushroom
Creamy Garlic
Fresh Tomato
Horseradish
Hot Salsa
Lemon Veloute

Marchand de Vin
Mustard Veloute
No-Peel Tomato
Quick Tomato
Sauce Robert
Sour Cream Gravy
Spicy Mustard Barbecue
Texas Sharp Barbecue

Lamb

Au Jus
Aurore
Basil Cream
Beurre Blanc
Beurre Rouge
Choron
Creamy Garlic
Curry Sauce
Fresh Tomato
Garlic Butter
Hot Garlic-Ginger

Lemon-Pecan
Lemon Veloute
Maltaise
Mango Chutney
Mango-Rum
Mediterranean Olive
No-Peel Tomato
Pan Gravy
Quick Tomato
Wild Mushroom

Liver

Apple-Onion
Brown Butter
Brown Mushroom
Curry Sauce
Fresh Tomato

Marchand de Vin
No-Peel Tomato
Normandy Apple
Quick Tomato

Pork

Apple Brandy-Cherry
Apple-Onion
Aurore
Buttery Ginger Barbecue
Classy Ketchup Barbecue
Dark Oyster Barbecue
Fresh Tomato
Hot German
Lemon-Orange Cranberry
Mango Chutney
Mango-Rum

Mediterranean Olive
No-Peel Tomato
Normandy Apple
Pan Gravy
Quick Tomato
Sauce Robert
Sour Cream Gravy
Sour and Sweet
Spicy Mustard Barbecue
Texas Sharp Barbecue

Veal

Au Jus
Basil Butter
Basil Cream
Buerre Blanc
Cream of Mushroom
Creamy Champagne
Fresh Tomato
Garlic Butter
Lemon-Pecan
Lemon Veloute
Maltaise

Mousseline
No-Peel Tomato
Normandy Apple
Pan Gravy
Quick Tomato
Sour Cream Gravy
Sweet Sesame Vinaigrette
Warm Anchovy
White Wine and Mushrooms
Wild Mushroom

FISH

Light-flavored Fish

Basil Butter
Beurre Blanc
Buttery Ginger Barbecue
Caper Veloute
Cream of Mushroom
Fish Veloute
Fresh Tomato
Garlic Butter
Hollandaise
Lemon Veloute
Maltaise

Meunière
Mousseline
No-Peel Tomato
Polonaise
Quick Tomato
Shrimp Butter
Sour and Sweet
Sweet Sesame Vinaigrette
White Wine and Mushrooms
Wild Mushroom

Medium-flavored Fish

Aurore
Basil Butter
Brown Butter
Creamy Garlic
Curry Sauce
Fresh Tomato
Garlic Butter
Hot German
Mediterranean Olive
Meunière

Mousseline
Mustard Veloute
No-Peel Tomato
Quick Tomato
Sour and Sweet
Texas Sharp Barbecue
Vegetable Vinaigrette
Warm Anchovy
White Wine and Mushrooms

Shellfish

Basil Butter
Béarnaise
Beurre Blanc
Clarified Butter
Creamy Champagne
Curry Sauce
Fish Veloute
Fresh Tomato
Garlic Butter
Hollandaise
Lemon-Pecan
Lemon Veloute

Maltaise
Mediterranean Olive
Meunière
Mornay
No-Peel Tomato
Polonaise
Quick Tomato
Shrimp Butter
Sweet Sesame Vinaigrette
White Wine and Mushrooms
Wild Mushroom

Smoked Fish

Basil Cream
Brown Butter
Caper Veloute
Clarified Butter
Creamy Garlic
Fresh Tomato
Garlic Butter
Horseradish
Hot German

Mediterranean Olive
Meunière
Mustard Veloute
No-Peel Tomato
Normandy Apple
Quick Tomato
Sour and Sweet
Spicy Mustard Barbecue
Texas Sharp Barbecue

POULTRY

Chicken

Apple Brandy–Cherry
Au Jus
Basil Butter
Beurre Blanc
Beurre Rouge
Classy Ketchup Barbecue
Cream of Mushroom
Creamy Champagne
Creamy Garlic
Creamy Red Pepper Puree
Curry Sauce
Dark Oyster Barbecue
Fresh Tomato
Garlic Butter
Hot Garlic-Ginger
Hot Salsa
Lemon-Orange Cranberry

Lemon-Pecan
Lemon Veloute
Mango Chutney
Mango-Rum
Mediterranean Olive
Meunière
No-Peel Tomato
Normandy Apple
Pan Gravy
Polonaise
Quick Tomato
Sour Cream Gravy
Spicy Mustard Barbecue
Sweet Sesame Vinaigrette
Texas Sharp Barbecue
White Wine and Mushrooms
Wild Mushroom

Duck, Goose, Turkey

Apple Brandy–Cherry
Apple-Onion
Creamy Red Pepper Puree
Curry Sauce
Dark Oyster Barbecue
Lemon-Orange Cranberry
Maltaise

Mango-Rum
Mediterranean Olive
Normandy Apple
Pan Gravy
Sour Cream Gravy
Sweet Sesame Vinaigrette

Game, Rabbit, Venison

Caper Veloute
Creamy Garlic
Curry Sauce
Hot German
Mango Chutney
Mango-Rum
Marchand de Vin

Mediterranean Olive
Mustard Veloute
Pan Gravy
Sour and Sweet
Sour Cream Gravy
Spicy Mustard Barbecue
Wild Mushroom

EGGS

Aurore
Béarnaise
Brown Butter
Curry Sauce
Fresh Tomato
Hollandaise

Hot Salsa
Mediterranean Olive
Mornay
No-Peel Tomato
Quick Tomato

PASTA, RICE

Alfredo
Aurore
Basil Butter
Cream of Mushroom
Creamy Garlic
Creamy Red Pepper Puree
Curry Sauce
Fresh Tomato
Garlic Butter
Goat Cheese
Hot Garlic-Ginger
Italian Meat

Lemon-Pecan
Lemon Veloute
Mango-Rum
Mediterranean Olive
Mornay
No-Peel Tomato
Pan Gravy
Quick Tomato
Sour Cream Gravy
White Clam
White Wine and Mushrooms

VEGETABLES

Artichokes

Basil Butter
Béarnaise
Clarified Butter
Garlic Butter
Hollandaise
Horseradish

Hot Garlic-Ginger
Lemon-Pecan
Lemon Veloute
Maltaise
Vegetable Vinaigrette

Asparagus

Beurre Rouge
Brown Butter
Clarified Butter
Hollandaise
Hot Garlic-Ginger
Lemon-Pecan

Lemon Veloute
Maltaise
Mousseline
Polonaise
Sweet Sesame Vinaigrette
Wild Mushroom

Beans, Chick-Peas

Curry Sauce
Hot Garlic-Ginger
Hot German

Lemon-Pecan
Mediterranean Olive

Bok Choy

Hot Garlic-Ginger
Lemon-Pecan

Lemon Veloute
Sweet Sesame Vinaigrette

Broccoli, Cauliflower

Brown Butter
Cream of Mushroom
Curry Sauce
Dark Oyster Barbecue
Garlic Butter
Hollandaise

Hot Garlic-Ginger
Hot Salsa
Lemon-Pecan
Mornay
Polonaise
Vegetable Vinaigrette

Cabbage, Brussels Sprouts

Curry Sauce
Hot German
Normandy Apple

Sour and Sweet
Vegetable Vinaigrette

Carrots, Parsnips

Brown Butter
Curry Sauce
Hot German

Mustard Veloute
Sour and Sweet
Sweet Sesame Vinaigrette

Celeriac, Celery

Mediterranean Olive
Mustard Veloute

Sweet Sesame Vinaigrette

Corn

Basil Butter
Curry Sauce

Mediterranean Olive
Sour and Sweet

Eggplant

Curry Sauce
Fresh Tomato
Italian Meat

Mediterranean Olive
No-Peel Tomato
Quick Tomato

Fennel

Basil Cream
Creamy Garlic
Fresh Tomato
Italian Meat

Mediterranean Olive
No-Peel Tomato
Normandy Apple
Quick Tomato

Green Beans

Brown Butter
Cream of Mushroom
Creamy Garlic
Creamy Red Pepper Puree
Fresh Tomato
Garlic Butter
Horseradish
Hot German

Italian Meat
Lemon Veloute
Mediterranean Olive
Mustard Veloute
No-Peel Tomato
Quick Tomato
Sour and Sweet
Vegetable Vinaigrette

Jerusalem Artichokes

Basil Butter
Brown Butter
Clarified Butter
Creamy Garlic
Creamy Red Pepper Puree
Fresh Tomato
Garlic Butter
Horseradish

Hot Garlic-Ginger
Lemon-Pecan
Lemon Veloute
Mediterranean Olive
Meunière
No-Peel Tomato
Quick Tomato

Jicama

Fresh Tomato
Mediterranean Olive

No-Peel Tomato
Quick Tomato

Leeks, Onions

Basil Cream
Beurre Rouge
Brown Butter
Creamy Garlic
Horseradish
Lemon Veloute

Mango-Rum
Mornay
Normandy Apple
Sweet Sesame Vinaigrette
White Wine and Mushrooms

Lettuce

Creamy Garlic
Hot Sake
Mustard Veloute

Sweet Sesame Vinaigrette
Vegetable Vinaigrette

Mushrooms

Basil Butter
Béarnaise
Creamy Champagne
Creamy Garlic
Garlic Butter
Goat Cheese

Horseradish
Hot Garlic-Ginger
Lemon Veloute
Mousseline
Warm Anchovy

Okra

Fresh Tomato
Hot Garlic-Ginger
No-Peel Tomato

Quick Tomato
Vegetable Vinaigrette

Peas

Aurore
Basil Butter
Basil Cream
Cream of Mushroom
Creamy Garlic
Curry Sauce
Goat Cheese

Lemon Veloute
Meunière
Mornay
Sweet Sesame Vinaigrette
White Wine and Mushrooms
Wild Mushroom

Peppers

Fresh Tomato
Hot Salsa
Italian Meat
Mediterranean Olive

No-Peel Tomato
Quick Tomato
Vegetable Vinaigrette

Potatoes

Brown Butter
Garlic Butter
Goat Cheese
Hot Garlic-Ginger
Hot German

Hot Salsa
Mornay
Pan Gravy
White Wine and Mushrooms

Pumpkin, Winter Squash

Brown Butter
Hot German

Lemon-Pecan
Sour and Sweet

Salsify

Creamy Garlic
Lemon Veloute
Meunière

Mornay
Wild Mushroom

Spinach, Greens, Radicchio

Hot German
Lemon Veloute
Sour and Sweet
Sweet Sesame Vinaigrette

Vegetable Vinaigrette
Warm Anchovy
Wild Mushroom

Sweet Potatoes

Brown Butter
Hot German
Lemon-Pecan

Normandy Apple
Sweet Sesame Vinaigrette

Tomatoes

Basil Butter
Goat Cheese
Hot Garlic-Ginger

Mornay
Vegetable Vinaigrette
Warm Anchovy

Turnips, Kohlrabi, Radishes, Rutabagas

Basil Cream

Vegetable Vinaigrette

Watercress

Creamy Champagne
Hot German
Lemon-Pecan

Vegetable Vinaigrette
Warm Anchovy
Wild Mushroom

Zucchini, Summer Squash

Basil Butter
Fresh Tomato
Italian Meat

Mediterranean Olive
No-Peel Tomato
Quick Tomato

DESERTS

Cakes

Butterscotch
Fresh Raspberry

Mango-Rum

Crepes

Cinnamon-Peach
Fresh Raspberry

Mango-Rum
Normandy Apple

Hot Fruits

Chunky Cherry-Nut
Cinnamon-Peach

Fresh Raspberry

Ice Cream

Butterscotch
Chunky Cherry-Nut
Cinnamon-Peach
Fresh Raspberry

Honey Hot Fudge
Mango-Rum
Rum Hot Fudge

INDEX